Midnight Marquee #78; Editiors—Gary J. Svehla and Susan Svehla; Graphic Design Interior—Gary J. Svehla; Cover Design—Susan Svehla; Copy Editor—Linda J. Walter; Contributing Writers—Anthony Ambrogio, Steven West, Gary J. Svehla; Acknowledgments—Warner Home Video; Fox Home Video; MGM Home Video; Universal Home Video; Bender Helper Publicity; Scott Essman; Publisher—Midnight Marquee Press, Inc.

Midnight Marquee #78
November 2011
Copyright © 2011 by Gary J. Svehla

Midnight Marquee Editorial

Published irregularly for $10 per issue by Midnight Marquee Press, Inc.

Articles and art should be transmitted electronically and will remain the property of the writer/artist and copyright holder, who will retain all rights. If material intended for publication is sent to us via regular mail, it is the sender's responsibility to include return postage. No responsibility is taken for unsolicited material.

Editorial views expressed by writers are not necessarily those of the publisher, Midnight Marquee Press. Nothing from the magazine may be reproduced or shared in any media without the expressed written permission of the publisher. The Midnight Marquee Press offices are located at: 9721 Britinay Lane, Parkville, MD 21234; website: http://www.midmar.com; e-mail: midmargary@aol.com

Letters of comment addressed to Midnight Marquee or Susan and Gary Svehla will be considered for publication, unless the writer requests otherwise.

Letters of comment are encouraged; please send all comments to midmargary@aol.com. Or you may send a letter to our editorial address.

We are always looking for writers to submit articles. Please discuss any article suggestions first with Gary J. Svehla at midmargary@aol.com and check the Style Sheet link on our website to get ideas of style and formatting. Length of articles may vary. We take them long and short. Remember, our emphasis is mainly on the classics of the Golden Age, but our definition of classic and Golden Age is not based upon specific decades or year of production necessarily. Instead it's the artistic content that reflects the heart and style of classic cinema.

Copies are mailed, within the USA, for the cost of the issue plus $1 for Media Mail; $6 for Priority Mail. Issues are sent in sturdy envelopes so they should arrive at your home in near mint condition. Foreign orders are welcome, but shipping costs vary. Check with us for pricing. We accept all credit cards, PayPal, checks and money orders.

Table of Contents

2 *Midnight Marquee* Editorial
   by Gary J. Svehla

3 *Alien*: In Space No One Can Hear Your Primal Scream
   by Anthony Ambrogio

16 A History of the Horror Film Portmanteau
   by Steven West

28 *Midnight Marquee* Book Reviews
   by Gary J. Svehla

30 *Midnight Marquee* DVD Reviews
   by Gary J. Svehla

This has been a sad issue to assemble. On May 21, 2011, my father Richard Svehla passed away from the effects of Alzheimer's at age 92. For years, even after he had retired from the magazine, Richard had been listed as Managing Editor. But he was so much more. After he encouraged me to publish my own fanzine as a 13-year-old Monster Kid, handling the finances and buying me hectographic and then mimeographic printing machines, he maintained "the office," which consisted of a typewriter, a box of index cards, envelopes and stamps. Dick seemed to take pride in receiving letters from enthusiastic readers and loved it even more when people telephoned him to sing the magazine's praises or voice complaints. And when we started doing shows at film conventions, setting up our displays, people anticipated our father and son combo. And he enjoyed that aspect the most. My father, who played the saxophone and keyboard his entire life, loved pressing flesh with people. Not only paying customers but also the interested horror and science fiction movie fans, people who wanted to shoot the breeze for a few minutes. He loved that. And people always seemed to love my father.

When we expanded the company and finally got serious, incorporating Midnight Marquee Press, Inc. in 1995 and expanding our line of magazines with a new array of trade paperback and case bound books, my father played a reduced role. My wife Sue had expanded the business with software programs and a rapidly multiplying inventory that meant my aging father was not able to run the business with a box of index cards any longer. The business had evolved beyond him, and Sue, who had the business sense in this family, took over. Yes, my father still attended many shows and manned the table, but even with his reduced role, he still enjoyed meeting friends and fans, promoting the merchandise and taking pride in the success of the business that he spawned with his Monster Kid Gary.

We stored all the back issues of the magazine at his house, and we were constantly phoning him to "dig out" five copies of *MidMar* #28 or asking him do we have reproduction copies of *Gore Creatures* #21? If we were out of repro issues (which were hugely popular), my father would gladly gather up the masters and drive to the photocopy shop and have new product printed up. He would do anything we asked of him and always took pride in helping us whenever and however he could.

At one of our FANEX conventions Sue and I decided to acknowledge him for all the years of hard work and dedication, by honoring him with an engraved plaque of appreciation. Of course it was to be a surprise presented at our annual Saturday evening awards presentation. Fred Olen Ray asked if he could be the one to introduce the award, as he always proclaimed my father to be the perfect dad for any horror movie fan. Most of the adult monster lovers would rant, including Ray, about how their parents never supported their love of all things horror and threw away their collectibles. But Fred Olen Ray always stated that he never met a parent who better supported the quirky eccentricities of his son. Others who knew my father concurred and I always agreed how lucky a son I had been. Ironically the night my father received his plaque and journeyed off to the bar to have people celebrate his lifetime of support, he left the plaque in the bar by mistake and it was never seen again. Apparently it was thrown out. But my father had a terrific night of celebration. If "Uncle" Forry Ackerman was our mentor, Richard was "the Father" that every Monster Kid wished he had.

Every single issue of *Gore Creatures* or *Midnight Marquee* published bears his personality and spirit. I started out as a kid who did not know anything about publishing and my father encouraged me. He handed over the reins to Susan, and we two have maintained the collective vision to this day. So, at the very least, we dedicate this issue to him and his memory, his spirit, his playfulness, his sense of fun and his devotion to a shy son's monster obsessions.

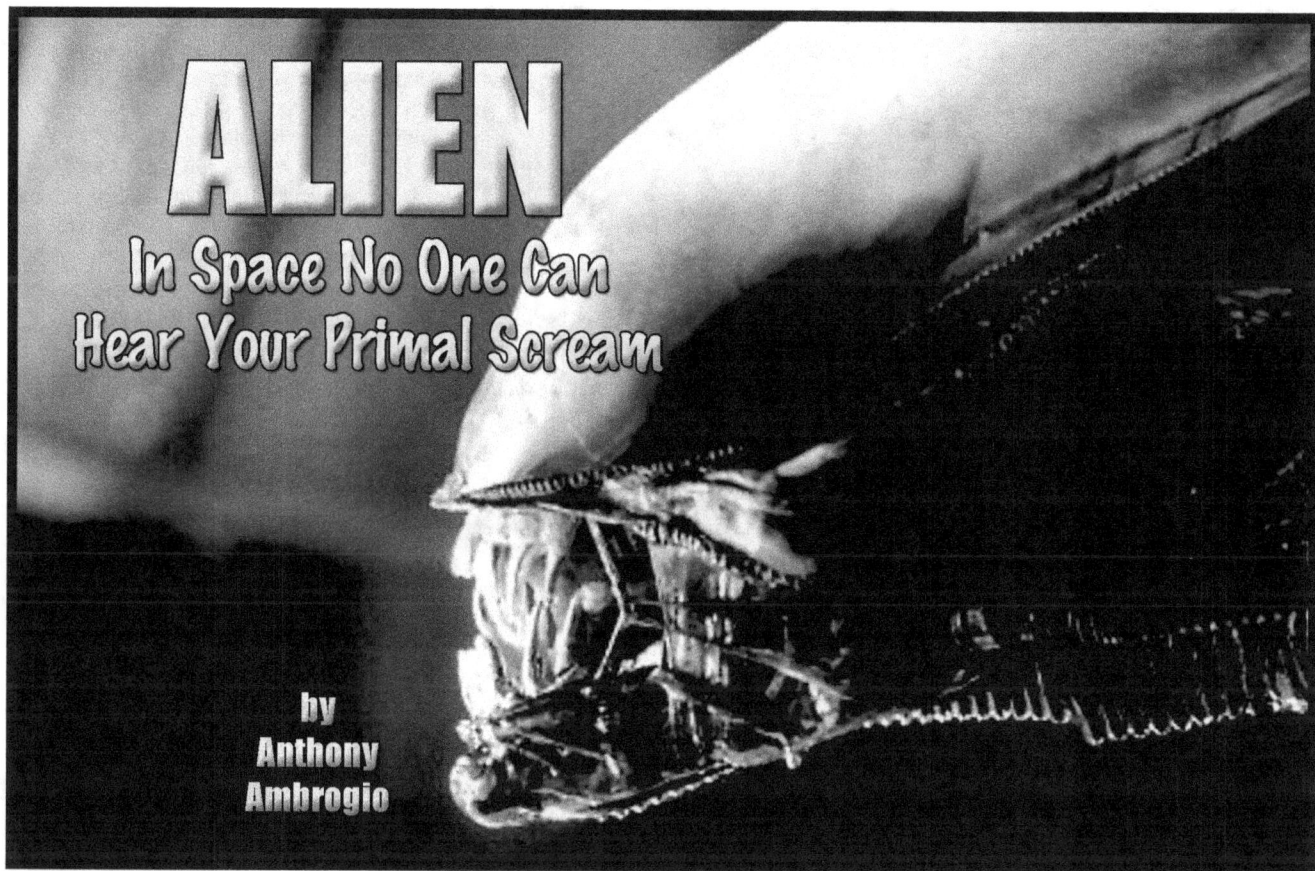

ALIEN
In Space No One Can Hear Your Primal Scream

by Anthony Ambrogio

0. Disclaimer

Some of us find it hard to believe that 2011 marks the 32nd anniversary of Ridley Scott's landmark science-fiction picture, *Alien*, which 20th Century Fox released on May 25, 1979 (exactly two years after the studio premièred George Lucas's phenomenal *Star Wars*, although it's hard to imagine two more different s.f. movies).

This article was originally presented as a paper at the Fourth International Conference on the Fantastic (Boca Raton, Florida, March 26, 1981). A shortened version appeared in *Eros in the Mind's Eye*, edited by Donald Palumbo (Greenwood Press, 1985). Since that time, there have been some major contributions to *Alien* studies, including David Thomson's book-length study, *The Alien Quartet* (Bloomsbury Publishing Plc, 1999)—not to mention the commentary that can be found on the various DVD issues of the *Alien* films. But none has ever looked at the movie the way that "In Space, No One Can Hear Your Primal Scream" does. Thus, for the first-time publication of the complete text of this article, I have, for the most part, used as references those articles and interviews that came out shortly after the movie played theatrically, as they have the advantage of "freshness"—of being critics' and filmmakers' initial thoughts before the sequels and many imitations got in the way.

You'll find frequent citations here from the following:

"Making *Alien*: Behind the Scenes," *Cinefantastique*, 9, (Fall, 1979). All references to this issue-length article are cited as "*CFQ*."

Steve Vertlieb's essay on *Alien* for *Cinemacabre*, no. 2 (Fall, 1979). All references to this article are cited as "Vertlieb."

Alex Eisenstein's "*Alien* Dissected," *Fantastic Films*, no. 13 (January 1980). All references to this article are cited as "Eisenstein."

Henry Golemba's "Not Quite So Alien," a paper presented to the First International Conference on the Fantastic in the Arts, March 1980. All references to this article are cited as "Golemba."

Donald Palumbo's "Loving That Machine; or, the Mechanical Egg: Sexual Mechanisms and Metaphors in Science Fiction Films," *The Mechanical God* (Greenwood Press, 1982). All references to this article are cited as "Palumbo."

Interviews with Ridley Scott, Tom Skerritt, Sigourney Weaver and Veronica Cartwright from "*Alien* from the Inside Out," parts 1 and 2, *Fantastic Films*, no. 11 (October 1979) and no. 12 (November 1979). All references to *Fantastic Films* are cited as "*FF*."

1. Introduction

Alien has sometimes been criticized for its apparent lack of solid characterization and its plot holes: Steve Vertlieb wrote, "*Alien*'s plot and script are its weakest elements" (Vertlieb, p. 26.2). Mark Patrick Carducci claimed that "*Alien* is out of balance, as long on forward momentum and shock as it is short on logic, depth of characterization or at times even clarity" (*CFQ*, p.13.1), Ivor Powell, *Alien*'s associate producer, called *Alien* "a hardcore adult cartoon" (*CFQ*, p. 32.3).

If this criticism is justified, why then is *Alien* such an effective movie? *Alien* director Ridley Scott claims "[*Alien*] works on a very visceral level, and its only point is terror, and more terror" (*CFQ*, p. 12.3). But what is the exact nature of that terror?

It is not simply *Alien*'s literal story of an isolated, trapped group of people struggling against some evil, awful force. After all, that formula is universal to horror films, from haunted-house tales of the 1920s to more recent *Alien* analogues such as 1951's *The Thing* (remade 1982) and 1958's *Thing*-inspired *It! The Terror from Beyond Space*. (Note the similarly inhuman concepts embodied in each title.) Nor is it the stylish way *Alien* is mounted and presented—though this, too, adds to its effectiveness.

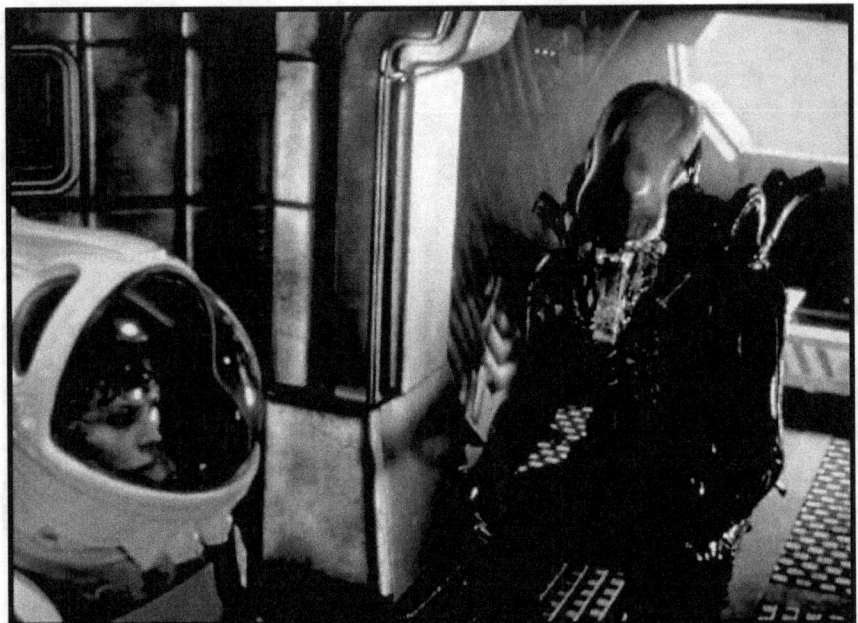

Terror in *Alien* is mounted from the sense of isolated, trapped people struggling against some evil force, a univeral theme in horror cinema.

However, if style were all (and I know I'm going to catch a lot of flak for saying this), Kubrick's *The Shining* (1980) and Scott's own *Blade Runner* (1982) would be better movies.

2. *Alien* as *Psycho*drama

Alien's structure is similar to that of *Psycho* (1960). Both films, criticized in their time for excessive gore and violence, actually contain little onscreen carnage, leaving the worst of it to the viewers' imagination—but both startle viewers with an early, unexpected outburst of violence (the shower murder, the chest buster), unsettling them, catching them off guard so they're always on guard and apprehensive after.

Voyeurism, perverse parent-child relations and sexually motivated murders appear in *Alien* as they do in *Psycho*—but in different form—and they are responsible for *Alien*'s "terror, and more terror," for its overwhelming impact.

Alien's images and events touch an archetypal, mythic nerve in us all—as most works of art that strive to be popular successes must do. But *Alien* contains no myth of the dying god, found in such films as *The Day the Earth Stood Still* (1951) and *E.T.: The Extraterrestrial* (1982), nor the similar religious iconography and theme of a *Close Encounters of the Third Kind* (1977). Instead, *Alien* is a double-edged nightmare: Embodying every child's worst fear, it frighteningly details the problems of siblings, supposedly secure in their parents' bosom (here, womb—the space ship as womb), suddenly thrown over by that parent and faced with a sexually aggressive, child-molesting ogre/penis/"father" (the Alien), who—having displaced them in their mother's affections—now seeks to exploit them, to introduce them to the most horrendous aspect of adult sex; violent penetration.

The W. H. Auden epigraph that *Alien*'s scenarists appended to their finished screenplay suggests that they knew they were tapping this particular archetypal nerve: "Science fiction plucks from within us our deepest fears and hopes, then shows them to us in rough disguise: the monster and the rocket" [quoted in *CFQ*, p. 13.1].

On top of this—because of this—*Alien* also depicts the first great and terrible journey we all must take, through the birth canal, for that is the only way *Alien*'s protagonists can break the now unsafe bond between their parent and themselves and (though ill-equipped to do so) prevent their violation by the Other.

In this scheme, the Nostromo crew members have dual roles, as children and as homunculi—unborn fetuses scurrying about the womb, waiting to be born, while some rough beast slouches after them. Caught between a rock[et] and a hard place—the penis and vagina in the throes of copulation—they're unwilling, unwitting, uncomprehending performers in a primal scene.

Others have treated, either in passing or in some detail, various aspects of this interpretation of *Alien*. For example, Vertlieb uses the crew-as-children metaphor—but as metaphor only. Eisenstein makes valid points about the sibling-Mother relationship and the rape motif but ultimately misinterprets their significance. Golemba articulates a number of important points about the crew as siblings, about Mother, rape and the film's climax, but often stops just short of making necessary connections and sometimes includes speculations that obscure his valid conclusions. And Palumbo insightfully details a number of *Alien*'s significant aspects, but only as part of a discussion of a dozen s.f. films, so his coverage is necessarily limited.

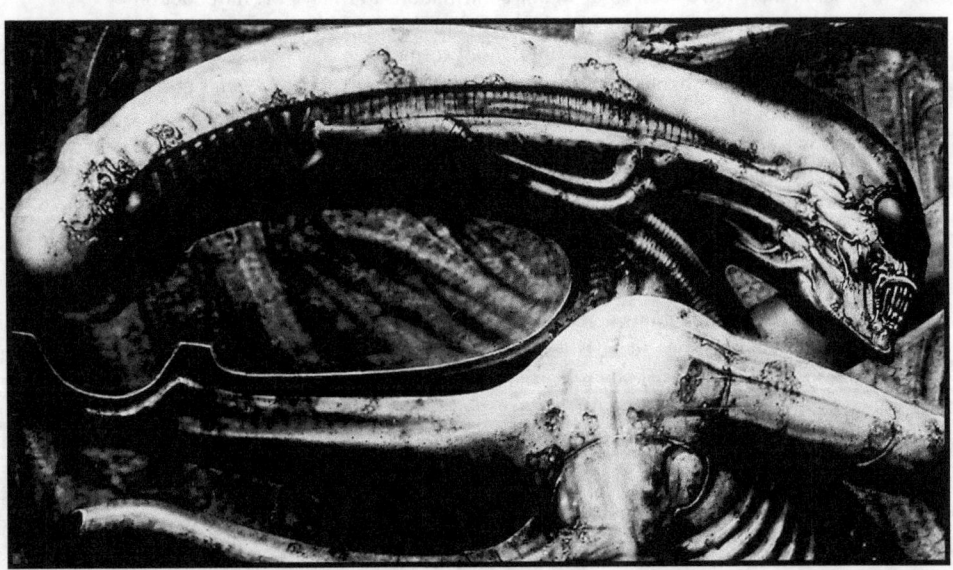

H.R. Giger's phallic art that inspired the look of the reproductive Alien.

Because no critic has seen or tied together all of the elements, they've often dismissed *Alien* as imperfect or ill-constructed.

3. Boys and Girls Together

That the Nostromo's crewmembers are children is evident. They are a close-knit family group; they interact as siblings do. See their meal-table sequences, and consider, for example, Yaphet Kotto's Parker, the literal black sheep of the bunch, who delights in annoying the others (probably his elder siblings because they occupy positions of authority over him) by pushing them as far as he can, usually seconded in his childish grievances (about the "bonus situation," about the time required to repair the ship) by his otherwise taciturn buddy, Brett (Harry Dean Stanton). The crewmembers' relationship to the computer, aptly named Mother, which controls the ship and their lives, is one of children to parent. They do not indulge in sex; they exhibit an innocence/ignorance/naïveté about it—especially when it comes to the cold, hard fact of the Alien itself.

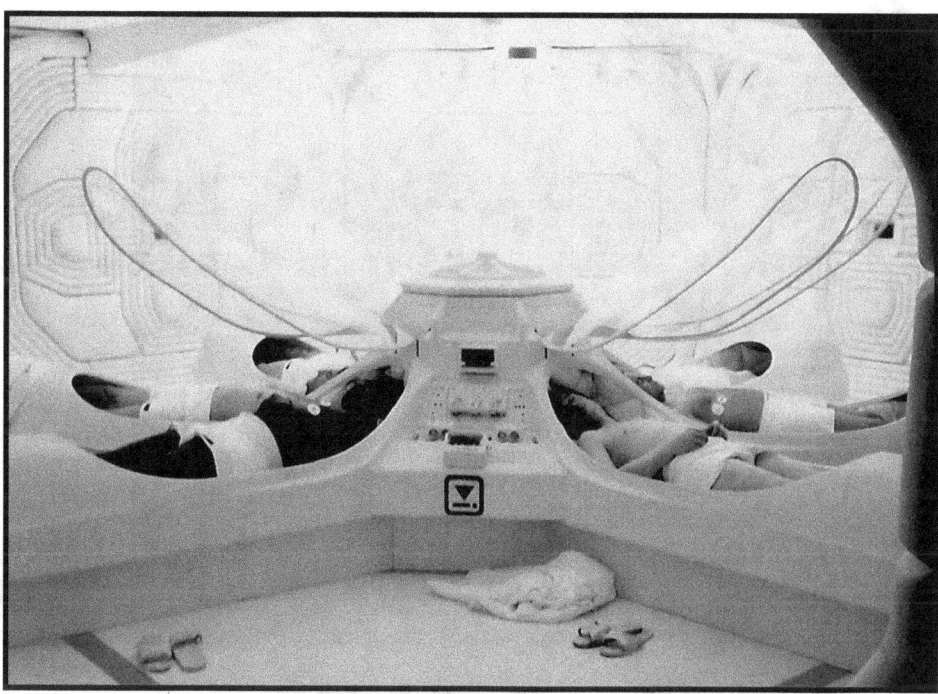

The Nostromo's crewmembers, innocent children, are awakened by Mother.

The Mother ship is the first "character" introduced in *Alien*. Scott's camera, panning across compartments and dollying down corridors, implies that the ship is a presence—a rather ominous one, as the shadowy visuals and murky background music combine to suggest. Mother, the computer who runs the ship (who *is* the ship, since only philosophically is there a split between brain and body) suddenly springs to life and makes her presence known, playing out her rapid thought processes on a telescreen.

To further convince viewers that Mother is a living entity, the visor of an empty space helmet facing the screen reflects these examples of her sentience—metaphorically anthropomorphizing the brains behind the crew, the intelligence that controls the ship. Then Mother awakens her children, innocently sleeping together in their room. The crewmembers' coeducational dormitory and unconcern about each other's undress upon arising underscore their childlike qualities and disinterest in sexual matters. Vertlieb's description of this sequence is useful for its telling imagery:

> Her systems activated by a distress signal emanating from an uncharted planet, Mother releases the slumbering technicians from their womblike bedchambers prematurely so that they may ... investigate the source of the emission. The[ir] sleeping quarters ... are white and sterile .... The crewmembers arise wearing only white sheets or bikini briefs. It is as though they are children awakening for the first time. Here in the simple shelter of this hospital environment, these children in space awake from ... primal innocence ... into a strange new world that they are entirely unprepared for. (p. 24.1-.2)

"Primal innocence," "womblike bedchamber," "released *prematurely*," "white and sterile hospital environment"—these and other phrases that Vertlieb uses are charged with a significance beyond the merely metaphorical.

The crew sleeps in one of the film's many wombs, in some sort of cryogenic state, and thus to be roused they must be warmed up. Therefore, the "womblike" beds act as incubators (which they physically resemble), reinforcing the hospital image but also relating the awakening to the idea of hatching, being born, coming into the world. (The bedchamber is a *nursery*: a place where children are cared for, a place where things are *grown*.) The crew is awakened, given birth, *prematurely*: The crewmembers are nowhere near the end of their journey—or their gestation—they're not yet ready to deal with the matters that now confront them. Their arising here is the first example of *Alien*'s several false/unnatural births.

4. A Monologue on Dialogue: Why *Alien* Contains So Much Baby Talk

Speaking of unnatural, from the beginning *Alien*'s dialogue had problems. Too wordy and artificial in Dan O'Bannon's original

Crewmembers explore the huge gun on the Alien planet.

While the women in *Alien* are not sexualized, sexual imagery abounds. Here the Nostromo crew enter a vagina-like opening on the Alien planet.

script (asserts Mark Patrick Carducci, who compared drafts; see *CFQ*, p. 16.2), the dialogue became too stark and cold in Walter Hill's rewrite. And David Giler's additions apparently made it too arch (according to Ivor Powell, *CFQ*, pp. 32.3-33.1). So the actors and director finally made most of it up as they went along. Tom Skerritt (Dallas), claims, "[The chest-buster scene] was all impromptu" (*FF* 12, p. 36.3), and Sigourney Weaver (Ripley), says, "We did a lot of improvising because the script was absolutely bare bones" (*FF* 11, p. 35.1). These largely impromptu reactions of the actors playing the characters resemble nothing so much as the gabbling or babbling of a bunch of kids. Like kids, the players were often reacting to hitherto un-experienced events (the most well-known example being the chest-buster scene—most of them didn't know what was coming).

The improvisational nature of *Alien*'s dialogue is apparent in the various characters' harping on one idea or another, in their childish (childlike) repetitions, which often dissolve into epithets expressing a child's frustration and rage. (Only Ash [Ian Holm], the fake human—the one who turns out to be a robot—has a good command of language, un-stutteringly articulating his lines—usually to confound the others with some scientific gibberish.) Certainly no one says anything profound or even quotable in *Alien*; the only memorable line is the extrinsic "In space, no one can hear you scream" of the film's ads, and the dialogue is largely either informational or inconsequential and banal, leaving the movie open to charges about its "comic-book" characterizations. But *Alien*'s dialogue and characterization actually work to its advantage because its characters are *not* complete; they are still unformed (and uninformed) children going through birthing and maturation processes which they only partly comprehend; as such, they are unable, unequipped, to say anything particularly intelligent about their experience.

5. Sex Differentiation in *Alien* (No Sex, No Differentiation)

Part of the lingering interchangeability or non-differentiation of the film's characters is perhaps due to the fact that, as originally written, *Alien*'s crewmembers were all male (see *CFQ*, p. 16.21). The sex change of the characters who became Ripley and Lambert (Veronica Cartwright) in the finished film came as a fortuitous afterthought on the part of the script's rewriters (see Giler, quoted in *CFQ*, p. 19.1), making for two female characters different from the usual helpless types found in s.f. films. Some critics still insist that Ripley and Lambert act like stereotypical s.f.-film females (Vertlieb, p. 26.2, Eisenstein, p. 58.1), but in the film their sex is never an issue, at least not for their fellow crewmembers. They're as scruffy-looking as their co-workers and share equally in all the shipboard duties, dirty work included. When Dallas chooses Lambert to be part of the detail to explore the derelict "bone" ship, he gives no thought to her status as a member of the "fairer" or "weaker" sex.

Later, Lambert's frightened passivity when the Alien is about to kill her is not due to her "femininity" but to her character. Throughout the film, she is the reluctant astronaut, always complaining. (When told to quit griping, she snaps, "I like to gripe.") She is never eager to go on a dangerous assignment—unlike the gung-ho Kane (John Hurt), who's first up out of hyper-sleep, first to volunteer for the expedition, first to find the Alien—and the first to be attacked by it. On the contrary, she's first to suggest abandoning ship after Kane is dead. That she should cringe, whimper, freeze in the face of the Alien is natural for her.

The women's unglamorous appearance and total participation in the crew's activities show that they are not aboard as sex objects, to service the males. They're not even the typical romantic leads, though Ridley Scott claims that Ripley and Dallas's "antagonism early in the story leads one to think (or hope) they'll wind up loving each other. " But," he quickly adds, "that's not the purpose of the film" (*CFQ*, p. 12.2).

Ripley's arguments with and concern for Dallas do suggest a certain special relationship between them, but she is to Dallas as Brett is to Parker. Third-in-command Ripley looks up to ship's captain Dallas as a younger sibling does to an older. She considers them both the sensible, responsible members of the family (as opposed to the irresponsible Brett and Parker and the indifferent others). She aspires to be like Dallas, to lead like him. And it hurts her when, in their argument about the Alien, he sides with Ash (the real misfit of the family).

Alien deserves its non-sexist due: On a literal level, its characters don't engage in sexual intercourse because they're professionals doing their job in an age when the close proximity of male and female doesn't automatically imply physical relationships. But, on a deeper level, the characters don't engage in sexual intercourse because they're children—they're *pre*-sexual. And because the crewmembers are at a pre-pubescent, non-sex-differentiated stage of development, the filmmakers allow the female members to be treated as/behave like, equals.

6. The Alien Penis: Sex Rears Its Ugly Head

One character in *Alien does* indulge in sexual intercourse with practically the entire cast: the Alien himself. His only purpose is self-preservation, self-perpetuation, self-reproduction, which he accomplishes through rape/penetration/violation. In all of his sentient incarnations he is almost pure phallus, although he makes his first appearance clothed in a passive-seeming, "female" form—the ovum, through whose labia he bursts forth, penetrating virgin explorer Kane's face-plate, Kane's hymen, and forcing himself down Kane's throat.

The filmmakers set up a metaphorical sexual penetration on the part of Kane and his companions and then violently reverse the thrust of this action, giving us actual sexual penetration from the supposed "female" element. Kane and company enter the bone ship through an orifice; he goes down into a uterine chamber and accidentally breaks the layer of light that houses the Alien's eggs. Since the Alien has previously penetrated the bone ship and raped its crew, it's logical that the derelict ship should be seen as a vagina, a womb, especially since it's carrying the Alien's eggs. (Compare *this* nursery to the Nostromo's.)

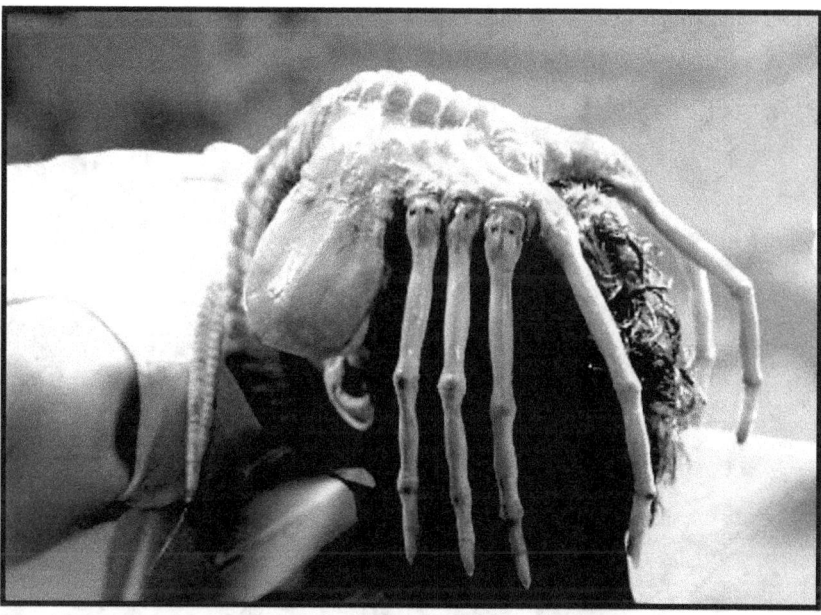

The Alien first seen as a grotesque claw, hugging and penetrating Kane"s (John Hurt) face, impregnating him with the alien seed.

In his first ex-utero appearance, the Alien is a grotesque claw, tenaciously gripping Kane's face, with a tail wrapped around his neck and another appendage thrust down his gullet (the ultimate "deep throat"). It is the grasping, groping, rapacious male reduced to his simplest components. And, once it implants its demon seed in Kane, its function is complete.

After a brief gestation period, Kane gives birth to the Alien's next form. That the chest-buster episode is an example of a horrendous Caesarian birth would be evident from the context, even without the outside confirmation we have for the scene. (For example, Scott referred to it at the time as "the 'chest-birth,'" *CFQ*, p. 12.2, and the dozens of films since then that have "borrowed" *Alien*'s eruption-from-within technique, have often depicted it as a grotesque, unnatural birth. Think of the belly-exploding births in *Humanoids from the Deep* [1980] and *Species II* [1998].) Because everything happens so fast here, perhaps a viewer hasn't the time to grasp this scene's implications, but the film spells them out later, after the now-grown Alien has killed Brett: "Kane's son," mutters Ash, referring, of course, to the Alien—whose masculine sex is *never* in question. Significantly, *Ash* is the one to voice this thought, since it turns out that he admires the creature and has affinities with it. (See section 9 below.)

Kane "bears" the Alien but is not its biological mother—merely a vessel (as women were always thought to be; compare the common description of a ship, a space ship, as a *vessel*). He is the host for the Alien's seed, the Alien's homunculus. "His" offspring shares none of his heredity but takes after its father, after itself, completely. And the Alien's infant form effectively expresses its essential personality/physiology: the ravenous, aggressive

The Alien is a survivor, which it accomplishes through rape/penetration/violation.

Midnight Marquee #78

and fitted in a distinctively organic rather than mechanical precision—that suggests a monstrously mutated side of beef more than the interior of a space vessel. (p. 121).

This idea is further confirmed by the Alien's designer, H.R. Giger, who—as everybody knows by now—designed the creature and various environments in the film "in order to achieve what I call my biomechanics" (*CFQ*, p. 35.2).

But back to the Alien, who gets bigger and stronger in practically no time at all. He seems to grow around, develop from his early penis shape, which apparently evolves into his protruding steel tongue with trap-shut teeth, dripping with lubricant—a tongue that swells whenever he's about to strike.

We might stop for a moment to ask just what that lubricant is that drips from his jaws. Is it saliva? Is it semen? Bolaji Badejo, the actor who played the Alien, claims, "They must have had about 2,000 tubes of K-Y Jelly … just to get the effect of the slime coming out of [the Alien's] mouth" [*CFQ*, p. 30.2]. K-Y Jelly is the product most frequently used as a lubricant in sexual intercourse. Was its use here coincidental or intentional? Whichever, its employment on the Alien's jaws is appropriate.

The android Ash (Ian Holm), becoming the subtle merger between the human and the mechanical, symbolizes H.R. Giger's concept of "biomechanics."

penis-as-weapon. ("I wanted it to be like an obscene phallic thing that was all mouth," says Scott [*FF*, no. 11, p. 34].) It skitters away, to hide until it's bigger and stronger—naturally gravitating to the Nostromo's airshafts, those corridors providing a natural habitat for the penis-creature: a snug, warm place in which to nestle and grow.

In Alan Dean Foster's novelization of *Alien*, when Ripley, Parker and Brett are hunting for what they think is the still-small Alien, Ripley unknowingly comes across evidence of the Alien's presence: "Ripley touched a wall accidentally, pulled her hand away in disgust. It was coated with a thick, viscous slime. Old lubricants, she mused" (*Alien* [New York: Warner Books, Inc., 1979], p. 199). *New semen*, probably—unless it's the Nostromo's own vaginal fluid flowing in the wake of the Alien's passage.

The bone ship, more visual evidence of the "biomechanical" look that Giger created for *Alien*.

I've touched upon the Nostromo's organic, womblike, female nature—a fact that the film confirms by the Nostromo's analogy to the other aircraft in the film, the derelict bone ship, which, as Palumbo writes, fully aware of his imagery's import, appears to have been grown rather than constructed; it is composed of huge interlocking bones, cartilaginous rings, Gargantuan filaments and membranes, and cavernous tracheal ducts—all asymmetrically shaped

His tongue, his tail and especially his head indicate his true nature—and literally what's on his mind. The Alien's form was inspired by two drawings in Giger's *Necronomicon*—"Necronom II" and "Necronom IV," a fact reported (e.g., see *FF*, no. 11, p. 17, and *CFQ*, p. 23.3) and instantly confirmed by one glance at both paintings. In fact, as Palumbo points out, "The Alien's head in 'Necronom IV' is even more pronouncedly phallic than is the head of the film's Alien, and 'Necronom II' has what are unmistakably erect penises instead of tongues protruding from its death's head jaws" (p. 122).

The Alien's appearance is in keeping with his function. Whenever we see him, he is almost always becoming engorged, erecting as the stimulus of his impending rape, penetration, excites him. His arousal is conveyed visually to the audience, mostly through its fear for his victims and once, perhaps, through its own sense of sexual arousal.

When Brett separates from the others to look for Jones the cat, horror genre convention dictates that he is doomed. It's just a matter of when. That "when" is excruciatingly put off. A similar kind of suspense occurs when Dallas, out of his element, pursues the Alien in *his* element: the airshafts.

Note producer Gordon Carroll's unconsciously sexually charged description of the film's suspense: "Yeah, … the anticipation. Harry Dean Stanton going after the cat, for example. And Tom Skerritt in the airshaft. We tried to stretch that band as much as we could. Because the anticipation is as thrilling as the moment, you know, even more thrilling" (*FF*, no. 12, p. 39.3). Carroll could be describing the creature's own feelings at these moments, particularly in the sequence that climaxes with Brett's death. The Alien quietly drops down and unfolds, expands, before Brett's terrified eyes. In close-up, Brett stares up at the now-enormous creature—the look on his face implying, "God, I never saw anything that *big* before!"—just before the Alien gives it to him.

At film's end, after Ripley escapes in the shuttle, something tells us the movie's not over yet, and again we wait with anticipation/dread —a dread increased and, perhaps, complicated by the fact that the falsely secure, innocent Ripley begins to undress here, leaving herself more open to attack and revealing for the first time (save for the fleeting unclear long shot when she and the others awoke) her woman's body underneath her unisex work clothes.

When Brett (Harry Dean Stanton) goes off alone to search for the missing cat, horror film convention dictates that he is doomed.

Henry Golemba suggests that, because Ripley's disrobing and half-nakedness represent the only image in *Alien* that could induce normal, *human* sexual excitement, "the movie invites the audience to be vicariously as monstrous for a moment as the alien" (p. 7). This contention provides another connection between *Alien* and *Psycho*, for, as Louis D. Giannetti says, "like many of Hitchcock's works, *Psycho* also deals with the idea of voyeurism—indeed with the idea of cinema as artistic voyeurism" (*Understanding Movies*, 3rd ed. [Prentice-Hall, Inc., 1982], p. 60). *Psycho*'s voyeurism has been often discussed and is now a commonplace of *Psycho* criticism. For our purposes, it's best to note that *Psycho*'s sexually troubled Norman Bates (Anthony Perkins) and *Alien*'s sexually ravenous Alien practice voyeurism.

To prove his point that Ripley's "strip-tease" is the only image that might induce normal sexual excitement, Golemba describes the scene in erotic terms:

> Ripley sheds her sexless fatigues and strips down to her underwear…bikini pants …. The camera lingers in a level frontal shot on Ripley's masked Venus mound, completely covered by a pure white triangle …. Her undershirt clings to her work shirt, lifts, and almost—maddeningly almost—exposes her left breast.
>
> Ripley pulls her shirt down innocently, unaware of the audience's voyeurism, and … bends over the [control] panel's right side, thus exposing half her anal cleavage, and stands there bent over for a long, long time. (pp. 7-8)

Ripley's strip is shot from a subjective point of view—the Alien's—which does put the audience in his position, thereby perhaps inviting it to share the creature's unnatural desire; however, although a viewer may see this scene through the Peeping-Tom Alien's eyes, s/he doesn't necessarily see it the *same way* as the Alien. Any cat-calls, whistles or other signs of arousal that some (male) audience members might exhibit here could be interpreted as phallus-to-phallus support for the Alien but would more likely represent the

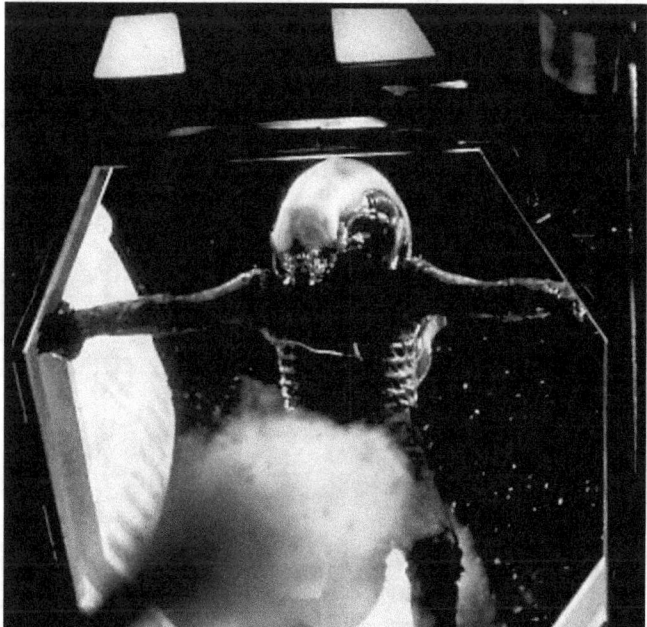

Before the Alien is thrust back into outer space, he had a subjective view of Ripley's (Sigourney Weaver) strip show.

Mother, the Nostromo's onboard computer, does not protect her "children" when she allows Ash to admit the alien contagion inside the space vessel.

audience's (false) relief from tension (similar to the nervous laughter sometimes heard after the chest-buster scene). I saw the movie in packed theaters three times, and I never heard any catcalls.

Golemba himself admits that viewer reaction here has more to do with concern over Ripley's vulnerability than lust for her body: "The audience grows quite silent at this moment, tension mounting in part because of anticipation of the hidden monster's appearance and in part because ... Ash ... tried oral rape [on Ripley] ... not so very long ago" (p. 8). In other words, the audience is fearful for Ripley, expecting an attack like the one she recently survived from Alien-emulator Ash.

The attack finally comes. Once again, the Alien grows, bloats, from his hidden position in—almost as part of—the ship. Apparently he's been nestling himself quite snugly among this craft's tubes and ducts, perhaps in a biomechanical attempt to fuse with it—so (especially since his excitement at the prospect of another potential victim is causing him to swell) it takes him some time to dislodge himself from the corner he's screwed himself into.

His protracted struggle to get free gives Ripley time to protect herself, clothe herself, gird her loins in impenetrable female armor (her own chastity belt), first by retreating to the cylindrical locker on board the shuttle and then by donning a self-sealing (virginal) spacesuit—womb within womb within womb—so she can repulse him.

Viewers who object to the seemingly protracted time it takes for the Alien to get free ignore the possibility of the Alien's fusion with the shuttle, of the clumsiness of a rigid and erecting member in a confined space and of the cinema's frequent use of the expansion of time, wherein editing—particularly cross-cutting, as here, between Ripley's preparations and the Alien's struggles—extends the length of an action that in real life would take much less time. Although the events depicted before the final confrontation occupy perhaps a minute or more of screen time, because of the built-up suspense, their actual duration may be much less.

After the preceding detailed examples, is it necessary to mention Lambert and Parker's violent deaths via the Alien's sexual contact? Both parallel Brett's to some degree: Lambert's fear, looking up, in the face of the growing Alien, and Parker's puncture by the creature's penis jaws.

Ridley Scott says, "I think finally, when you want to be really scared, you've got to have a very private thought. You've got to think about what it is that physically makes you very uneasy, that upsets you in a primal way" (*CFQ*, p. 14.3). That's what the Alien does to most people. Considering the crewmembers' position as children, the Alien's monstrousness must upset them in a primal way. What could be more terrifying and less understood than a pure, unadulterated, potent phallus, especially to a bewildered child who sees it in action and can think of it only as a dangerous bludgeoning weapon that hurts, kills?

7. Mother Invents Necessity, Necessitates Invention

Perhaps the only thing more terrifying and less understood by a child is its mother and her own genitalia, her own sexuality, especially when the outsider, the invading penis, triggers that sexuality. This is the case with Mother in the movie. Throughout her children's ordeal, she never seems to protect or help them. In fact, she is responsible for that ordeal, apparently acting on orders from "the Company" (perhaps *her* "id" or "libido"?). She has her children act as her "go-between," procuring the Alien for her. (We'll take up this idea of "the Company" in section 8.)

Note that the side trip to the storm planet to investigate the signal and ultimately to pick up the Alien is another of the picture's

false births. When the crew detaches itself from the main ship to go down to investigate the planet, Ripley's voice [n.b.] can be heard announcing "Umbilicus clear." But Mother is still with them when they land—Ripley communicates with her—and, of course, they return to Mother's apron strings shortly after.

From the beginning, Ripley doesn't want to admit the Alien; she wants to follow the established quarantine procedure, probably obeying every mother's standard standing order about not opening the door to strangers. So Mother must subvert her obedient child's scrupulousness by having unscrupulous Ash sabotage Ripley—open the door and let the interloper in.

Later, when Dallas requests assistance from Mother to combat the Alien, she tells him she's "unable to compute," and, when he asks, "What are my chances [of survival against the creature]?," she tells him that his question "does not compute." Her children cannot understand why she and science officer Ash are unable to help them against the intruder. (Mothers are supposed to know everything, after all.) "Mother and I are still collating," Ash tells Ripley after the third death—which, under the circumstances, makes *collating* sound like some obscene, incestuous activity.

Along the way, the crew is confronted with a series of mysterious mechanical malfunctions. For example, the Alien-tracking devices prove unreliable at crucial times. "One is tempted to blame shoddy equipment," says Alex Eisenstein, "because other answers are not provided" (p. 60.1). However, the answer is not shoddy equipment, as Eisenstein sarcastically suggests, but a conspiracy of machines (controlled and led by Mother, seconded by Ash), all in collusion with the Alien, protecting it.

8. The Plot Coagulates

Alien's major plot "malfunction" surfaces when it's revealed that Ash, to the crew's detriment, is one of the machines protecting the Alien.

Ripley (Sigourney Weaver) confronts Ash, who is one of the machines protecting the Alien.

Certainly the accidental acquisition of the Alien and even the ship's subsequent protection of and preference for him are believable, possible occurrences that require no explanation. But the revelation that Ash is a robot, assigned to ensure the creature's return, introduces an element of premeditation that confuses the issue and raises unanswered questions. Parker asks, "How come the Company sent us a goddamn robot?" Ripley replies, "All I can think of is they must've wanted the Alien for the weapons division. [Ash has] been protecting it all along."

But this explanation is woefully inadequate. If the Company knew the creature's actual potential, why entrust its retrieval to an untrained crew ill-equipped to deal with the threat it posed and probably unable to get it home in one piece? But how *could* the Company know the creature's true potential? And, if it didn't, why take such radical, lethal steps to preserve it? And so on, around and around it goes.

Eisenstein, who raises objections similar to mine (p. 54.3), further comments, "That [Ash] turns out to be a robot stooge is a surprise because his status as stereotype scientist and ordinary company stooge seems sufficient in most ways to cover his previous behavior" (p. 58.2).

Ash *was* just a devious human in an early Walter Hill draft of *Alien* (see *CFQ*, p. 14.2), but he became a robot in a subsequent Hill-Giler rewrite; for one reason, because the scenarists thought it was a clever "boffo" idea—the kind that catches an audience off guard in an unexpected way (see *FF*, no. 12, p. 60.2). The other reason was because Hill had also introduced and given a large role to Mother, and the filmmakers feared

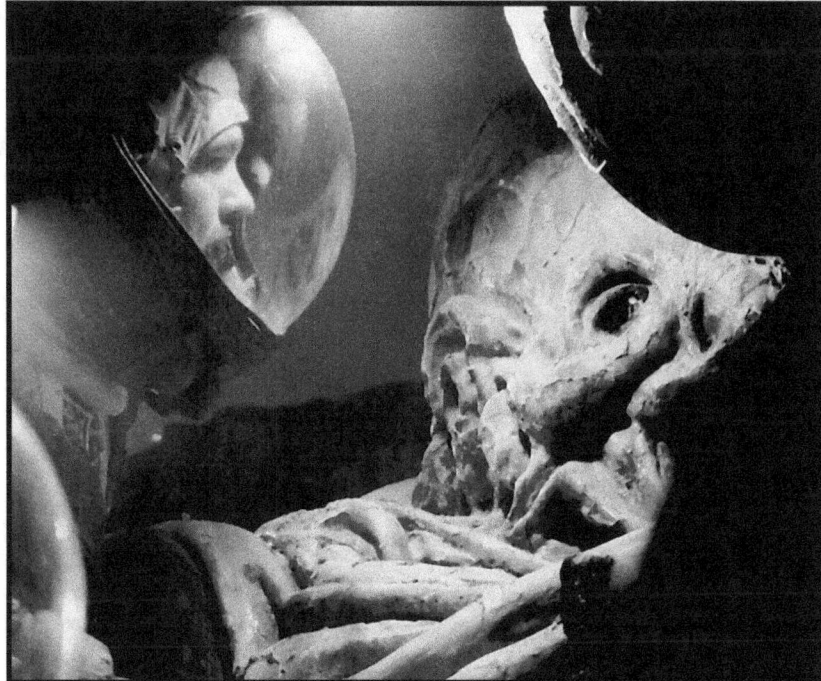

Dallas (Tom Skerritt) examines an alien life form while the crew explores the alien breeding planet.

The Nostromo crew (left to right): Ian Holm, Sigourney Weaver, Tom Skerritt and John Hurt

its personality and the scripted events associated with it made it too much like the famous computer in *2001: A Space Odyssey* (1968).

In Hill's early script, the very vocal Mother has no foreknowledge of the Alien and doesn't want him for any weapons division. Instead, she regards the struggle between crew and Alien as an experiment in the survival of the fittest and says, "In the interests of pure scientific research, I removed myself from the struggle" (see *CFQ*, p. 17.2, for the complete excerpt). And, just as Bowman (Kier Dullea) performs a lobotomy/robotomy on the unhinged HAL in *2001*, so too does Ripley perform an emergency hysterectomy on Mother (see excerpt, *CFQ*, p. 17.1, and the text below for a discussion of its implications).

This draft, containing Mother's clearly articulated reasons for guarding the Alien and the more direct Mother-daughter conflict, seems thematically "cleaner," more overt, than the filmed version. Despite the appropriateness of this aspect to the story, it was altered. "The parallels to *Space Odyssey* were just too close. So we broke Mother down into Ash," says Ridley Scott (*CFQ*, p. 14.2). This change obscures motivation in *Alien* but reinforces its theme of the crew as children, for, when we realize that children are not equipped to, cannot possibly fathom their parents'—adults'—sexuality, then the paradox of how the Company (that entire world of authority out there) could know about the Alien without knowing becomes understandable in view of the crew's/children's ignorance of sexual matters—and the line "All I can think of is they must've wanted the Alien for the weapons division" becomes not a "crucial explanation … tossed off in a perfunctory manner," as Eisenstein thinks (p. 54.1), but a revealing symbolic/thematic statement on how the crew sees the Alien and what he represents (the penis as weapon).

9. Ash into Ashes, Lust to Rust

While viewers would probably have no trouble believing that a *human* Ash would behave as the robot Ash does, in terms of the film, it's important that Ash be separate, different, from the real humans on the ship. Given his actions, it's only right that Ash should be allied with, similar to, the Alien and Mother—the film's other biomechanical characters. Ash is not a real kid like the rest of the crew—he's a midget, sexually aware, more sexually advanced than his brothers and sisters, in league with Mother and envious/emulous of the Alien, whom he protects. We never see Ash ever really threatened by the Alien, and he doesn't meet his end at its hands—because they are two of a kind. He's defeated by the humans, as is the Alien (and Mother, in her own way).

His end comes as he is engaged in a very Alien activity—trying to murder Ripley through forced fellatio. This sequence begins on a note of sibling rivalry. After Ash again feigns ignorance about the Alien, Ripley tells him, "I've got access to Mother now, and I'll get my own answers, thank you." She enters the ship's inner sanctum, the womb of wombs, the privileged place where previously only eldest child Dallas has been permitted. Her experience there is even more frustrating than Dallas's was earlier, for she finds that Ash seems to have gotten to Mother before she has. ("Special order 937" is "for science officer's eyes only.") In desperation, she punches at the keyboard and finally gets Mother to admit her dark secret about the Alien ("Insure return of organism ... All other considerations secondary. Crew expendable.")

At this point, thoroughly dejected because she's been thoroughly rejected by her parent, she's confronted by smirking Ash, whose seemingly effortless penetration of this area mocks the elaborate ritual she (and Dallas before her) had to perform to gain admittance. In no mood to listen to his unctuous reasoning, she lashes out at him, which unbalances him, causing him to strike back at her by imitating—in a way, *becoming*—the Alien he so admires, tossing her around and trying to shove a rolled-up magazine down her throat. (From a glance at the pin-up pictures on the wall behind, the viewer suspects that the weapon Ash uses is probably a porno magazine. There's a certain metaphorical appropriateness to his action: using an object in which women are generally treated as objects in his treatment of Ripley as object.)

The rolled magazine is Ash's surrogate penis, which is fitting for Ash, the surrogate Alien. His sterile violation here, which can only result in Ripley's death, clearly hearkens to the Alien's own oral rape of Kane, which resulted in Kane's death and the Alien's issue. Luckily, Parker and Lambert come to their sister's aid and bash Ash into submission.

10. A Love Only a Mother Could Face

Ash's spectacular death, commencing when his head's knocked off (talk about an image of castration!), was, as mentioned, originally planned for Mother. Armed with her own surrogate phallus, a screwdriver, Ripley crawls inside Mother's most private part and starts stabbing at a series of "raised crystals. Each glass dome containing amber fluid" (Mother's ovaries), smashing the glass and spilling the fluid all over (cf. Ash's ejaculations when he's decapitated), while Mother alternately screams at and pleads with her child ("You bitch," "You little cocksucker," and "Don't, baby [*n.b.*]. Don't"), at the same time removing all the air from the compartment (denying needed nutrients/oxygen which the placenta supplies), making Ripley struggle in a vacuum—the void created by the withdrawal of parental love (see the excerpt from Hill's draft, quoted in *CFQ*, p. 17.1).

Though this confrontation among Mother's electrical circuitry underlines Ripley's Electra complex (from Greek literature, the daughter's supposed attraction to her father), it is simpler than the film's more complex working out of that conflict, and it also requires Ripley to act inhumanly, to employ the Alien's means and method to defeat her foe—a kind of weapon and method she rarely uses in the film. Ripley doesn't destroy Mother in the movie until almost the end, when she programs the ship to *self*-destruct, to use its own force against itself. Even after initiating the self-destruct sequence, Ripley has a hard time going through with it and leaving Mother, especially when the Alien blocks her passage to the escape shuttle. In order to save herself, she feels she must reverse the process, exercise the override option.

In the film's most nerve-grating moments, she seems to succeed at the task, just in the nick of time, but, ignoring her infant's efforts, Mother dispassionately continues her countdown (in the cultured British voice of Helen Horton—the only time in the film when Mother speaks). This is more than Ripley can bear. She feels like a child betrayed, punished even though she's behaved herself and performed all her chores: "Mother! I've turned the cooling unit back on. *Mother!*" Ignored, unanswered, Ripley lashes out physically and verbally, futilely and impotently, trying to hit, to hurt Mother, calling her "You bitch!" (the same epithet Ripley hurls at the Queen Alien in *Aliens* [1986]), to no avail. There is nothing left for Ripley but to try to make it to the shuttle and get away on her own. Sigourney Weaver says:

> The thing I thought was the most interesting about Ripley when I read the script was here's a woman who lived her life very much by the book and believed that rules existed for a reason. But, when the alien appears, there's nothing in the book to go by, and she has to react only from instinct, and that's very hard for her. (*FF*, no. 12, p. 34.1-.2)

Ripley believed in the sanctity of the womb, the inviolability of the family unit, but she learns the hard way after the Alien's invasion that one can't be a kid forever and one can't go home again, can't return to the womb.

Certainly, Mother seems heartless and unfeeling in her final rejection of Ripley, but again this is because we are seeing events from the child's perspective. At this point, Ripley cannot understand that her Mother must force her to go out on her own, loose the apron strings, cut the umbilicus—give Ripley birth as her own person. That's why the self-destruct process isn't negated: Mother knows she must let Ripley distance herself from her, lose her dependence on Mother, even if this amounts to destroying the Mother to save the child.

Ripley's Caesarian birth here is analogous to Kane's delivery of the Alien, but it's the only *true birth* in the picture—an act Ripley both desires and fears. If Ripley (and the others) cannot comprehend Mother's sex life, Mother's preoccupation with the Alien, she certainly cannot figure out this necessity for separation—at least

Three crewman wander down the corridors of the alien-infested Nostromo, the humans literally wandering down the birth canal awaiting their transformations.

not until much later, when she's grown up. For this is no gentle Lamaze method; here is the birth trauma pure and simple (maybe not so simple). Those screaming klaxons, strobing lights and streaming gases, representing the anguish of labor pains for Mother and child alike, cannot be denied or stopped once set in motion.

The split-screen explosion, marking the Nostromo's destruction, is "feminine" in appearance: labia opening to expulse a child; cf. the split-screen vaginal tunnel of light that Bowman travels in *2001* (see Palumbo, p. 122). Eisenstein describes this action correctly but misinterprets its meaning:

> When Ripley rushes back to make amends, to cancel the destruct sequence, she must go through the entire procedure in reverse…, like some mystic rite or ancient formula of apology. And even this does not appease Mother, who puts a time limit on such things, and so her daughter is cast into the outer darkness to content [sic] with monsters alone. (p. 62.1)

It may seem like that to Eisenstein, to Ripley certainly—probably to everyone born of woman—but that's life! One must face "monsters" on one's own.

11. You've Come a Long Way, Baby

There remains one last thing Ripley must do to prove she's her own person and can stand up on her own, especially since her birth/ escape from Mother is not entirely an act of her own volition. Now in her own shuttle, her own womb, she must once again meet and this time defeat the Alien on her own, by herself, in this place. And that's what she does, in the manner previously, partially, described in section 6 above.

Note that Ripley uses "feminine" means to reject/dispel/discharge the Alien, resorting only briefly to anything phallic, anything "alien." After clothing herself in her own egg, her own shell, she straps herself in her chair and depressurizes the cabin (the "female" strategy Mother uses on her in Hill's early script), forcing the Alien almost out of the shuttle door. To get him out completely, she must fire the grappling hook at him, but—and this is a significant irony—her use of this phallic instrument allows him to hang on, to climb back up the outside of the rocket and attempt one last penetration through the shuttle's exhaust. Ripley steps on the gas, fires her resistors, and resists his advances, employing Newtonian physics in the form of a stellar douche to rid herself of the creature for good. (The material used to create this effect underlines its virginal/vaginal triumph: "We used water for the exhaust effect," says Scott, "…I wanted that whiteness [for purity?]" [*CFQ*, p. 14.1].)

Some critics complain about this final triumph on "aesthetic" grounds, claiming the "unrealistic" look of the Alien as he floats in space and attempts to clamber up the rocket destroys the carefully built menace his appearance has hitherto inspired:

> After two hours of brief, teasing glimpses …, this is really the first time that the audience is given an opportunity to study the creature as a whole, with realistic perspective. The effect is disillusioning. As the alien bounces clumsily about from portal to portal, it takes on the appearance of a tiny, awkward rag doll, its arms and legs flying carelessly into space … there is an undeniable feeling of disappointment and dissatisfaction … this rather obvious and disarming view of a not-so-alien Alien can only distract an audience and remove much of

the disgust and revulsion felt toward the creature quite effectively seconds before. (Vertlieb, p. 29.1-.2)

Perhaps at the end, when its humanoid silhouette is briefly seen in full as it clambers up a rocket nozzle, it suddenly loses its great and terrible strangeness, becomes too prosaic in its all-too-human shape and movement. (Eisenstein, p. 56.1)

There is, of course, a practical explanation for the Alien's non-threatening, even comical appearance here. Ridley Scott says they only had a day and a half to shoot the scene and "what's seen on screen is the test. We used the test!" (*FF*, no. 12, p. 59.2). But the Alien's appearance here is entirely appropriate and in keeping with the story. The point is that the repulsed, vanquished Alien *should* look weak and ineffectual, flaccid and small, at this moment. His threat has been dissipated; he has been shut out and so shrinks to minuscule proportions (is revealed, perhaps, for what he is—just a prick).

With this victory, Ripley is inviolate, whole, her own person. She has freed herself from two types of adult tyranny, seeming and real (with a little help from the adult in the former case), midwived her own rebirth, and can now curl up in a womb of her own and sleep the sleep of the innocent.

The film's last image, probably *Alien*'s only comforting shot, is a slow zoom in on Ripley in her sleep case, a sleeping beauty (Giler: "We wanted a *Sleeping Beauty* ending," *CFQ*, p. 20.2), ready to be awakened by a kiss, able—because of her experience—to face the real world, to engage in a proper sexual relationship when the right person comes along. In this, *Alien* is reminiscent of *2001*, which ends with the star-child's return to Earth in its floating womb. But, although the birth metaphor is very much a part of *2001* (see Palumbo, pp. 122-123), it is more appropriate here—because the birth is earned, deserved, because it is coupled with other elements of survival, because *Alien* is a fetal coming-of-age story.

12. Afterbirth

It turns out that Ripley *was* a sleeping beauty—although she's not awakened by a kiss. In James Cameron's exciting sequel, she's discovered—not 100—but 57 years later, and she continues her development as a person, this time becoming a surrogate mother herself—the adoptive parent of little Newt (Carrie Henn).

If we read the *Aliens* novelization or see the extended cut of *Aliens*, we also learn that Ripley has already *been* a biological mother: she left a 10-year-old daughter behind when she went on her voyage in *Alien*. While her mother was asleep in deep space, this 10-year-old aged and died (at 67!—apparently, even though these films are set in the far future, human longevity has decreased). This information was no doubt an after-the-fact addition to Ripley's back-story, one the scriptwriters thought would add more poignancy to Ripley's attachment to Newt, making that attachment a "redeeming action" for our hero. (It would also have complicated some of my interpretation of the first film had it been "known" then.) But, of course, in the finished *Aliens*, as originally released, the filmmakers chose to eliminate this "fact." It was enough that Ripley the "child" of *Alien* matured into Ripley the mother of *Aliens*.

Unfortunately, starting with *Aliens*, the filmmakers took too literally the idea of "the Company" wanting the Alien for its weapons division—the central paradox of the first film that can only be explained symbolically. In *Aliens* and the subsequent sequels, the idea of the big corporation striving to use the Aliens as the ultimate fighting machine became a major plot point and a matter of faith.

Leaving that aside, at the end of *Aliens*, Ripley has squared off against that other Mother and (using similar "feminine" methods to those she employed in *Alien*) has saved Newt, "her" child. She also appears to be on track for a proper sexual relationship with the right person, Michael Biehn's Hicks. All three of them participate in another *Sleeping Beauty* ending.

Veronica Cartwright and John Hurt seem concerned, being trapped on a claustrophobic spacecraft harboring the seeds of their destruction.

The less said about David Fincher's *Alien³* (1992) the better. In *You're Next! Loss of Identity in the Horror Film* (Midnight Marquee: 2008), Arthur Lundquist's superb entry points out the betrayal that *Alien³* perpetrates on its audience—callously eliminating Hicks and Newt before the picture even begins, for expediency's sake, then subjecting Ripley to numerous indignities and killing her off at the end.

It would have been better if *Alien³* were treated like that second (or was it the third?) season of *Dallas*—which turned out to be all a dream—so we could ignore it. Although Joss Whedon didn't do that when he scripted *Alien Resurrection* (1997), he did the next best thing, using the stupid ending premise of *Alien³* (that Ripley was impregnated with an Alien "embryo") to (re)create a Ripley who's part Alien and then giving her a *grand*child in the form of the humanoid Alien offspring who kills its Alien mother and whom Ripley must kill in a scene that is both terrifying and wrenching.

A History of The Horror Film Portmanteau

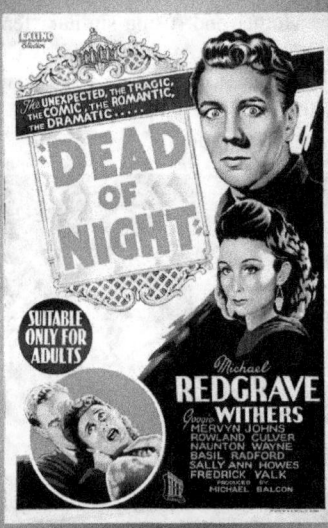

By Steven West

Michael Dougherty's *Trick 'r Treat* (2007) finally made its way onto DVD in October 2009 after being unceremoniously shelved by distributor Warner Bros. By virtue of being very, very good, it has quickly found its way into the hearts of horror fans, despite its lack of theatrical release. As well as being that 21st century rarity—an original, witty new horror movie—Dougherty's film accumulated affection for its revival of an enduring subgenre of horror, the anthology or portmanteau. By its very definition, the horror portmanteau offers value for money by presenting three or more individual stories, usually linked by a framing story, which itself has a sting in the tale. Horror has often worked best in its shortest form and the anthology format is a testament to that fact. On the basest level, if you're not digging the story you're currently watching, you'll always know another one will be along in a few minutes. (Sometimes this backfires. In the case of the ill-conceived *Creepshow 3*, the worst thing being the realization that there'll be more stories to come.)

The format is almost as old as cinema itself. Among the earliest examples of the portmanteau film are Germany's 1919 *Eerie Tales*—which, like subsequent anthologies *Unusual Tales* (1949) and *Master of Horror* (1960), takes significant inspiration from Edgar Allan Poe (specifically *The Black Cat*, which became the middle segment of Poe-based portmanteau *Tales of Terror* from Roger Corman in 1962). Fritz Lang's *Destiny* (1921), although not overtly a horror movie, set the tone for things to come with its twisting, influential framing story featuring Death spinning three yarns. 1924's *Waxworks*, incorporating appearances by Ivan the Terrible and Jack the Ripper, and Julien Duvivier's glossy Hollywood Oscar Wilde adaptation, *Flesh and Fantasy* (1943), also offer early templates of what would become a regular genre structure.

The most famous of all the initial attempts at a multi-story horror film is easily Ealing Studio's justly celebrated *Dead of Night* (1945). One of the few British horror films of significance in the barren pre-Hammer decade (yet, ironically, put out by a studio renowned for its droll comedies), this popular post-war compendium opens at a very British country house, where Mervyn Johns' account of an unsettling, recurring dream inspires shared spooky experiences. Overseen by four different directors, *Dead of Night* features five sinister tales—a short opener about an ominous bus conductor, a memorably chilly Christmas ghost story at a children's party, a simple but eerie haunted mirror tale and a lightly comic golfing ghost story, featuring Basil Radford and Naunton Wayne, that tends to get short shrift from even the movie's biggest admirers.

The best of the stories possess a marvelous anecdotal quality and generate the pleasant, nostalgic spine-shivers you may recall from listening to an elderly relative tell ghost stories to you as a child or sneaking downstairs to watch a creepy re-run of *The Twilight Zone*. The abiding memory of *Dead of Night* for most viewers, however, is the final story that takes the film into more psychologically unsettling territory. Ventriloquist Michael Redgrave's command over his unnerving dummy Hugo seems to slip and lead to homicide in an episode that remains filmdom's most enduring creepy-dummy horror story, despite stiff competition from the underrated *Magic* in the 1970s. The power of this story and the cleverness of the movie's cyclical, still-influential twist helped make *Dead of Night* a success,

though it took the worldwide success of Hammer's Gothic revival to bring about a return of the episodic format, with the additions of color and a greater frankness about sexuality and violence.

In the middle of his AIP/Poe cycle, Roger Corman produced the likable trifle *Tales of Terror* (1962), notable mostly for giving Vincent Price full rein to steal the show as the star of three separate adaptations of Poe stories. *Morella* and *The Facts in the Case of M Valdemar* skew toward a somber, straight horror aesthetic, but *The Black Cat*, one of an endless series of movie versions of the tale, is largely played for broad laughs and, like the subsequent *The Raven*, is dominated by a comic double-act between an inebriated Price and Peter Lorre. Price again essayed multiple characters for 1963's Nathaniel Hawthorne–inspired *Twice Told Tales* and would return to the horror anthology format for his penultimate genre film, the overlooked *The Offspring* (1986).

The 1960s elevated the horror portmanteau to the level of cinema art thanks to the work of esteemed directors like Masaki Kobayashi, Frederico Fellini and Roger Vadim, whose contributions came in the eerie form of *Kwaidan* (1964), a prototype and precursor of what would become known as J-Horror in the 1990s, and the colorfully bizarre *Spirits of the Dead* (1968). Arguably Mario Bava's *Black Sabbath* (1963) became both more endearing and effective as a pure horror portmanteau than either of those.

Typical of Bava's oeuvre, the movie offers playful misdirection at the start, with genre legend Boris Karloff playing himself as a campy Crypt Keeper figure warning the audience directly, "I hope you didn't come to the movies alone," before reminding us that vampires and ghosts also go to the movies. Karloff's framing scenes, and indeed the hilarious post-modern gag at the very end, pre-figuring the final scenes of both *Blazing Saddles* and *Monty Python and The Holy Grail,* are in contrast to the serious, intense tone of the three stories that unfold. Unlike the Amicus portmanteau movies that were to come, Bava opts for straight scares and psychological terror.

The Telephone, in which well-stacked brunette escort Michelle Mercier is menaced by recurring, increasingly threatening phone calls, is the only non-supernatural tale in the trio and, like Bava's subsequent *Bay of Blood*, predicts what would become slasher movie clichés, including escaped-lunatic red herrings and the use of the telephone as an instrument of terror. Given what is to follow, though, it can't help but look like a saucier than average episode of *Alfred Hitchcock Presents* by comparison.

The Wurdulak, a masterful exercise in Gothic horror on a par with Bava's *Black Sunday*, gives Karloff his creepiest ever screen role as a missing patriarch who may or may not have joined the ranks of a legendary bloodthirsty vampire known to superstitious locals as the Wurdulak. Before the final shot is engulfed by fog, this atmospheric story yields at least one enduring nightmare image (one that would be quoted in Stephen King's *Salem's Lot*)—a freshly buried, undead small boy pleads "Let me in" at a character's window.

The third story, *The Drop of Water*, has corpse-desecrating nurse Jacqueline Pierreux menaced at home by a fly, by persistent drops of water and, ultimately, by the grotesque cadaver itself, wearing a fixed post-mortem grimace that would be blackly funny if it weren't so terrifying. This, too, is a *tour de force* of horror filmmaking, with brilliant use of sound and framing.

Some of this writer's earliest memories of watching horror movies as a kid growing up in a country with four TV channels (three

Midnight Marquee #78   17

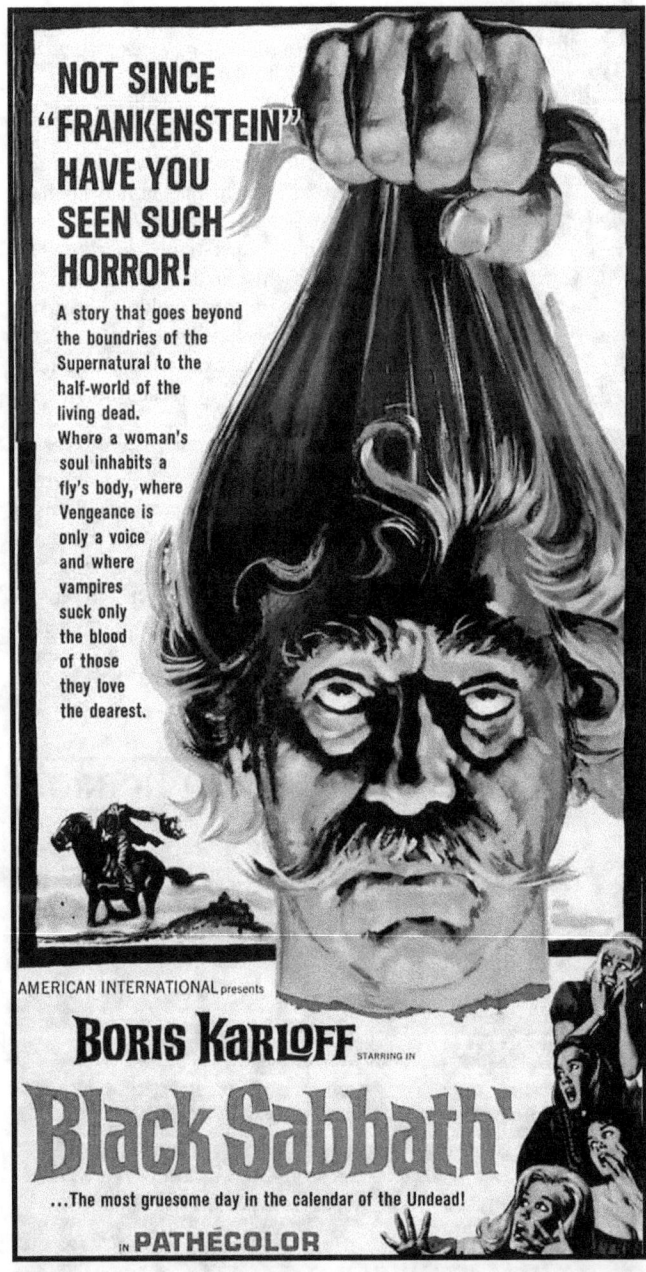

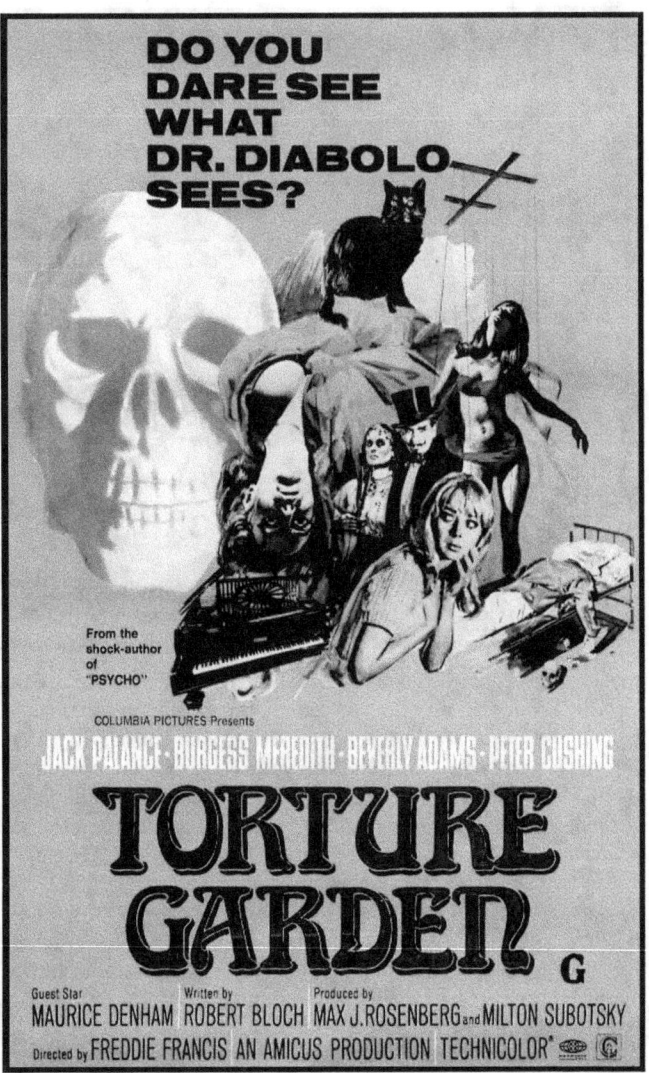

before 1982!) involve the BBC's late night movie schedules, which invariably featured something made by either Hammer or Amicus. The format of the horror anthology, for at least a decade, belonged to the latter—a little British production company founded by two Americans who, in attempting to wrestle some business from the world-dominating Hammer Film Productions, made the portmanteau their stock in trade following the success of their initial foray, *Dr. Terror's House of Horrors* (1965). Not nearly the best of their cycle, this trendsetter was mild enough to only warrant a PG rating in the U.K. and was nonetheless a lively and likable portent of things to come. The package has what would become a standard framing device. Peter Cushing's tarot-reading Dr Scheckall eyebrows and hammy German accent to back up his homage-to-*Nosferatu* moniker foretells the grim destinies of five train passengers before a twist reveals him to be The Grim Reaper.

The yarns spun by Dr. Schreck encompass everything from ambient she-wolf Gothic horror to light-hearted vampirism (featuring a young Donald Sutherland), with a somewhat embarrassing pre-political correctness voodoo tale and a marvelous crawling-hand riff on *The Beast With Five Fingers* (featuring Christopher Lee at his snotty best as a condescending art critic) in between. For British viewers, the enduring highlight might well be *Creeping Vine*, in which well known MOR radio personality Alan Freeman returns from holiday to discover his house is now under the command of a potentially world-domineering, invincible mutated vine. A brief but deliciously silly variant on *Day of the Triffids*, the segment gets a high curio factor for Freeman's presence. If you're American, just imagine a killer plant movie with Casey Kasem (host of *America's Top-Forty*) as the deadpan hero.

Cushing's ominous host and the eerie, much-imitated twist ending are perhaps the strongest suits of the first Amicus anthology, and both were recycled in the movies that followed, including the weaker *Torture Garden* (1967), in which Burgess Meredith's carnival barker Dr. Diabolo (you'll guess who he really is after around five minutes) oversees stories of Hollywood robot celebrities and murderous grand pianos. Cushing has roles in both this and *The House That Dripped Blood* (1970), also scripted by Robert Bloch, with a thick streak of self-referential humor apparent from the start as real estate agent Mr. Stoker (John Bryans) recalls the past horrors of a foreboding country house.

Peter Duffell's old-fashioned, bloodless (despite the title) movie has an opening story that foreshadows Stephen King's *The Dark Half* and a subtly sinister tale of juvenile witchcraft entitled *Sweets To The Sweet* that cleverly subverts Christopher Lee's sinister screen persona. Continuing a horror anthology trend to save the best till last, however, it's *The Cloak* that may have been even more fun with Lee in the lead role. This is the one with Jon Pertwee as a frustrated horror star who buys a 13-shilling cloak from cat-stroking eccentric Geoffrey Bayldon (in a wonderful pastiche of Ernest Thesiger's Dr. Pretorious from *Bride of Frankenstein*, complete with arched eyebrows). Consequently Pertwee turns into a vampire for real while filming *Curse of the Bloodsuckers*, a parody of Hammer movies featuring dodgy model work and Ingrid Pitt's cleavage.

Bloch returned to write the even stronger *Asylum* (1972), with a wraparound story stolen for the later *Tales That Witness Madness* (1973), in which medic Robert Powell conducts a movie-long search for the elusive "Dr. Starr," a member of the staff now apparently masquerading as a patient at the eponymous nut-house. Darker than most Amicus anthologies, the movie opens with the terrific *Frozen Fear*, which allows Bloch to indulge his fascination for corpse disposal (originally represented in *Psycho*), as adulterous Richard Todd buys his domineering wife a new freezer so he can hack her to bits and store her in memorably neat brown paper bundles that come to life in a droll, surreal climax.

Barry Morse is *The Weird Tailor*, assigned to make a very specific suit for grieving father Peter Cushing's dead son and, like a lot of Cushing's early 1970s horror roles, the actor (who lost his beloved wife Helen in 1971 to cancer) invests his much publicized real-life sadness into a melancholic character driven to extremes by the death of a loved one. *Lucy Comes To Stay,* somewhat similar to *Trilogy of Terror's Millicent and Therese,* has a staircase stabbing similar to *Psycho*'s, while *Mannequins of Horror* is a superior precursor to *The Puppet Master* franchise with a terrific Herbert Lom as the creator of an army of living dolls modeled in his own image, complete with internal organs. The punch line of *Asylum* is one of the best of the Amicus run and allows Geoffrey Bayldon to deliver what might be the craziest laugh in British horror, prior to a typically tongue-in-cheek knowing wink to the audience at the very end.

The most famous of Amicus' multi-storied horrors is *Tales From The Crypt* (1972), which, along with *Vault of Horror* (1973), displayed the most overt influence from EC Comics' infamous line of gleefully ghoulish horror comics. The former is the best movie the studio ever put out and, in the EC tradition, doles out grisly justice to foolish and unpleasant people. Ralph Richardson is a dour but articulate Crypt Keeper foretelling the fates of five travelers before we realize they are already in Hell as a result of their deeds.

The classic *And All Through The House* unfolds on Christmas Eve, the merriest time of silly hats, endless carols on the radio and unfaithful wife Joan Collins offing her boring husband with a fire poker before a homicidal maniac in a Santa suit shows up. *Poetic Justice* has another outstanding Cushing performance as Arthur Grimsdyke, a good-hearted, widowed garbage man driven to suicide by a hate campaign but returning from the dead one year on. *Wish You Were Here* is a truly grim, mean-spirited variation on *The Monkey's Paw* in which Barbara Murray's wish for wealth is granted at the expense of her husband's life. When she wishes him back to life, he gets the delight of eternal agony thanks to the embalming fluid running through his veins. All of these are gruesome, well-acted horror stories with pitch-perfect twist endings, and the final story, *Blind*

Alleys, sums up the overall tone quite nicely in the choice given to the Scrooge-like director of a home for the blind. He can either face a starved band of ravenous German Shepherds or run down an unlit, narrow corridor lined with razor blades.

Vault of Horror has its own memorable facets. Terry-Thomas inadvertently pulls on a pair of wife Glynis Johns' big pink knickers before she bludgeons him to death in *The Neat Job*. The pre-*Omen* creative deaths at the heart of *Drawn and Quartered* feature

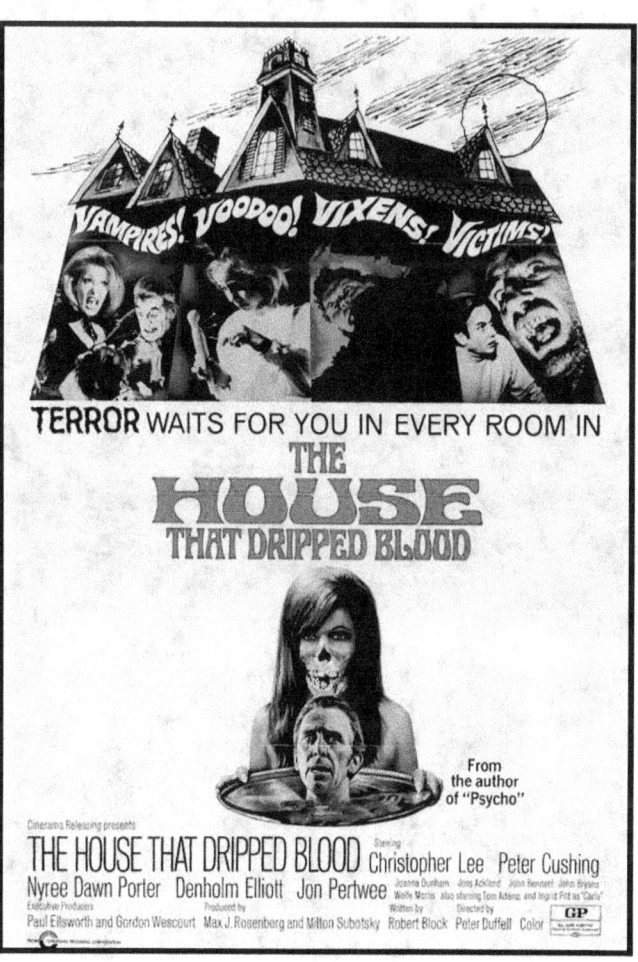

Patrick Magee (as Dr. Rutherford) is attacked by killer mannikins from *Asylum* (1972), one of Amicus' most popular portmanteau.

another erstwhile *Doctor Who,* Tom Baker, as an intense artist using his paintings to avenge those who have wronged him. *Tales That Witness Madness* (1973) is unforgettable for *Mel,* a parody of soap opera marital-strife plots in which constantly nagged Michael Jayston leaves (and kills) his wife for a tree that shows him more love and desire than she ever did. The most British of the entire cycle is Kevin Connor's underrated *From Beyond The Grave* (1973), with a lovely Cushing turn as a Yorkshire antique dealer whose dishonest customers meet sticky ends via the items they purchase. In the latter a characteristically intense David Warner becomes a hooker-killing slave to a demonic mirror that demands "Feed me blood" a là Audrey II from *Little Shop of Horrors,* while Margaret Leighton is hilarious as a dubious, mad medium ("half price on Thursdays!"). The second story is one of the most darkly funny and subversive of the whole Amicus line and has an extraordinary Angela Pleasence as the odd daughter of chummy, henpecked ex-serviceman Donald Pleasence, who, prior to a sour *Bay of Blood*-style twist, is dominated by a brassy wife (Diana Dors) who constantly mocks his job and manhood.

Amicus eventually found its brand of horror was far too quaint and modest to compete with the visceral box office hits of the *Exorcist*-era, and their anthology cycle petered out with the minor *The Uncanny* (1977). Cushing appears again and the movie features lots and lots of cats. Roy Ward Baker's goofy but likeable *The Monster Club* (1980) followed. There's something very charming about the fact that, in the year that *Friday the 13th* made a fortune, a company still raised money for a flick that ends with veteran vampire Vincent Price grooving down on the dance-floor to a track called "Fangs For The Memory."

The late Dan Curtis dominated the genre on the small screen in the 1970s, fresh from the success of *Dark Shadows* and the two

excellent (TV series-spawning) *Kolchak* movies. Curtis was also at the helm of two significant small-screen horror portmanteau movies.

The one everyone remembers is *Trilogy of Terror* (1975), which bucks the trend for wraparound stories in horror anthologies and simply lets three Richard Matheson terror tales unfold, connected only by the fact that each one stars Karen Black in a different role, given a rare showcase for her versatility. In *Julie* she's a dowdy, workaholic teacher who turns the tables on a cocky student and makes a credible transition from downtrodden spinster to seductive serial killer. *Millicent & Therese* revolves around a fashionable post-*Psycho* twist in its tricky tale of twin sisters, allowing Black to play both a mousey loner and a provocative, cruel femme fatale in a shag-me skirt.

Black has the final, classic segment *Amelia* all to herself, save for a voice on the phone. A prominent influence on everything from *Child's Play* to *Gremlins* (a kitchen attack ends with the aggressor oven-baked), *Amelia* has Black as a professional woman alone in a sublet city apartment menaced by a living, malicious Zuni fetish doll intended as a gift for her boyfriend. The absurd premise is rendered with terrific use of special effects, camerawork and a succession of devastatingly effective moments including the disappearance of the doll's tiny knife and the sight of a small shadow scurrying across the apartment, etc. It also has one of the most sinister fade-outs in all 1970s horror: The Zuni-possessed Black waits with a big knife for her mom, grinning with a mouth of Zuni-esque pointy teeth.

Curtis' later *Dead of Night* (1977), again in collaboration with Matheson, also has a knockout ending as part of a stand-out final story, though in this case it's preceded by unremarkable tales of a

time-travelling car (*Second Chance*) and Patrick Magee doing some eyebrow acting in the playful *No Such Thing As A Vampire*. The stand-out is *Bobby*, in which Joan Hackett uses black magic to bring her teenage son (Lee Montgomery) back from the dead, the boy returning with weirdly unsettling questions and an all-too eager desire to play an intense game of Hide and Seek.

Bobby is a story educated in the be-careful-what-you-wish-for school of horror, with a potent *Monkey's Paw* influence, and, like *Amelia,* centers around the sustained terrorization of a lone woman in her house against an unlikely but relentless enemy. For TV horror, it's remarkably grim and subversive in its suggestions of the kind of a mom Hackett was to Montgomery when he was still alive. Also in its scenes with Mom repeatedly shooting her "dead" child, we again question her maternal instincts. Few anthology horror punch lines are as harrowing as this one's. Right before the nightmare-inducing final reveal, the line, "Bobby didn't like you, so he sent me instead" will never fail to get those long-suffering neck hairs standing to attention.

Two decades later, Curtis returned to the well, directly remaking *Bobby* and sequelizing *Amelia* as part of the ill-conceived *Trilogy of Terror II* (1996), with Lysette Anthony no match for the underrated Black. Now and again, a TV network delves into the realm of anthology horror, usually with so-so results like Joseph Sargent's *Nightmares* (1983), which features characters menaced by a Satanic black truck, a giant rat, the old killer-in-the-back-seat urban legend and (ye gods!) an early 1980s arcade game. Douglas Jackson's

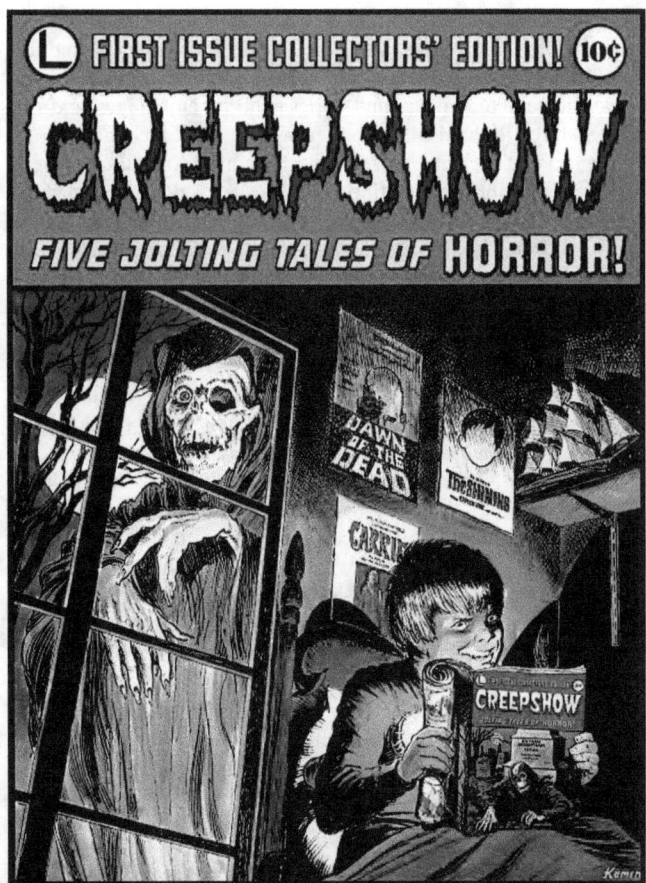

Twists of Terror (1997), in spite of an effective wraparound involving wigged-out hermit Joseph Ziegler, is a weak urban offering. Equally mundane, the Clive Barker/Stephen King double-act *Quicksilver Highway (*1997) tried to establish a characteristically manic Matt Frewer as a fresh Crypt Keeper-ish horror host.

The best TV genre anthology of recent times was the unpretentious but fun *Body Bags* (1993), in which co-director John Carpenter relishes his role as a wisecracking corpse snooping around a morgue before his autopsy and finding the three body bags with the juiciest stories to tell. Carpenter's *The Gas Station*, a suspenseful riff on his own *Halloween* slasher set up, with new employee Alex Datcher beset by weirdoes before a serial killer (Robert Carradine) strikes; and *Hair*, a very funny mad doctor satire with Stacey Keach going to extreme lengths (even using David Warner!) to avoid baldness, hit all the right scary/comic notes and are first-rate examples of the form.

It's entirely fitting that the resurfacing of the horror anthology theatrically was instigated by Stephen King, whose work was often indebted both to EC Comics and specific movies like *Dead of Night's* creepy episode, *Bobby*. King's first original screenplay was for George Romero's loveable *Creepshow* (1982), which from the outset captures the gaudy primary colors and gruesomely tongue-in-cheekiness of its printed page inspiration beautifully.

The Creep—just part of Tom Savini's extensive make-up effects work on the movie—is the ghoulish host of five stories, though animation and a live-action framing story involving King's own kid as a horror-loving brat with a horror-hating dad punctuate the movie.

Father's Day, the opener, is a typical *Tales From The Crypt*–style tale of money-grabbing bastards getting what's coming to them, and the segment is notable for Ed Harris' groovy dancing, a great worm-ridden ghoul ("I want my cake!") and the least sympathetic movie characters of 1982 (and that was the year of *Amityville II!*).

Good-natured silliness and gamely cartoonish acting are also characteristics of *The Lonesome Death of Jordy Verrill*, in which an incredibly broad King has his mouth permanently set to the agape setting as a dumb farmer stereotype stumbling into a 1950s sci-fi scenario that turns him into a suicidal man-plant. *Something To Tide You Over* has more stars, including Ted Danson as a brown-trousered lothario claustrophobically buried up to his neck at the beach by chuckling sadist Leslie Nielsen, following his wife's marital indiscretions. This one generates genuine creeps thanks to the clever use of 1980s CCTV camera technology. One has to love the ominous image of an eerie mist creeping into the frame of one of the black and white monitors, heralding the arrival of two seaweed-covered zombies.

The bloodiest episode is *The Crate*, in which hen-pecked schmuck Hal Holbrook uses a bitey, hairy monster to finally get rid of his obnoxious drunk wife. In a show-stopping moment, the unrepentant bitch (Adrienne Barbeau) even finds time to mock Holbrook's sexual failures while she is about to be eaten. And the one with the highest rewind factor in the VHS era was *They're Creeping On You*, a *tour de force* in which grumpy germophobe E.G. Marshall's $3200-per-month penthouse is overrun with roaches. The stark white set design is startling in contrast to the garish colors of the previous stories, and the eruption of bugs from Marshall's head and body at the end provides a great moment of repulsive 1980s body horror.

Creepshow helped inspire a fresh rash of horror portmanteaus throughout the decade. Romero returned (but without Stephen King)

to script the less stylish, cheaper but still fun *Creepshow 2* (1987), a movie hurt by tacky animated skits, but one that features two excellent nasty stories—*The Raft*, with a notably unpleasant oily trash bag-like monster melting the skin of one-note teenage protagonists, and *The Hitchhiker*, in which a persistent hit-and-run victim spends 20 minutes taunting the heartless woman (Lois Chiles) who left him as road kill, featuring the memorable line, "Thanks for the ride, lady!"

King's other stab at the anthology format was a lot milder than all of the above—the PG-13 rated *Cat's Eye* (1985), styled as a vehicle for a pre-teen Drew Barrymore, containing a vertigo-fueled suspense thriller named *The Ledge* and a bland, soppy finale entitled *The General*, in which a child's bedroom becomes the battleground for a breath-stealing troll and hardy cat. The first story, *Quitters Inc.*, however, has a terrific James Woods as a New York businessman who participates in Alan King's intense quit-smoking program, which involves family cats electrocuted to the tune of "Twist and Shout," his daughter abducted, and his wife threatened with rape. It's a neat satire and there is one splendidly surrealistic smoke-dominated nightmare sequence set to the sinister beat of The Police's "Every Breath You Take."

At the lower-budget level can be found occasionally clever items like *Screamplay* (1983), *Deadtime Stories/Freaky Fairy Tales* (1986), featuring Cathryn DePrume as a sexy homicidal Goldi Lox, and the unique *Night Train To Terror* (1985). The latter is especially interesting given that it was re-edited from existing, unfinished/obscure feature films with a funny framing device in which God (billed as Himself in the credits) and Satan (Lu Sifer) argue about the human race during a train journey (Satan: "I offer adultery, alcohol, cocaine, greed … that's why you're losing so many!") and decide on the fate of three characters. The individual stories are a hotchpotch of Poe homage, stop-motion animation and god-awful 1980s break dancing, but there's a demented energy at work, especially in the fascinating third tale, about an elderly Jewish concentration camp survivor who claims an ageless Nazi is the Anti-Christ building a new culture based on the belief that God is dead.

The best horror anthology of that decade that taste forgot is arguably Jeff Burr's 1986 shocker *The Offspring*. In the final years of his career, Vincent Price is fittingly cast as a master storyteller, an enigmatic librarian telling reporter Susan Tyrell of his Tennessee town's bloody history and chewing over lines like, "It's as though the very foundation of this place was human suffering," with that distinctive Price relish. The four stories that follow are remarkably consistent for a format that usually throws up equal parts wheat and chaff.

The opening segment has a suitably sad, pathetic Clu Gulager as a mild-mannered loner driven by rejection to murder a co-worker he loves and, worse still, screw her corpse at the funeral home. Nine months later he stabs his own sister in a very 1980s exploitative bathtub scene right before a grim newborn turns up at his house ("Daddy!"). Not quite as sick but even gorier is the third tale, a visceral shocker focused on Carney performer The Incredible Arden, who eats anything (razorblades, glass, sprouts…) and suffers the consequences when he is cursed by his community for running away from the Carney with a girl. Grueling gore special effects result, as screws protrude from his fingernails and razors slice him open from the inside, shards of glass slashing through his chest.

The unrelentingly grim tone is reinforced by the final story, a harrowing riff on *Who Could Kill A Child?* but set at the end of the

Civil War. Cameron Mitchell's band of Confederate soldiers pay for their callous actions when captured by a gang of orphaned kids who have turned to violence after seeing all the adults killed during the war. The story is weakened by some of the juvenile acting, but otherwise it contains remarkably powerful stuff for an R-rated genre flick; this underrated low-budget movie is also memorable for Price getting his most graphic onscreen demise since *Witchfinder General*, following a drunken toast to Edgar Allan Poe, a cute homage to his evergreen 1960s Corman-Poe cycle of films.

The 1990s were not a fruitful time for horror in any domain, and the horror anthology format largely lived on via the small screen in the form of HBO's *Tales from the Crypt* and assorted seasons of *The X-Files*. Most horror movies limped out straight to video, including disposable anthologies like 1991's *Campfire Tales* (not to be confused with 2001's *Campfire Stories)*, with Gunnar Hansen as a yarn-spinning hobo sharing tame riffs on urban legends and old Crypt episodes. The one exception was the little seen *Grim Prairie Tales* (1990), a genuinely atmospheric horror Western with four serviceable stories. For once the framing story (featuring a bickering, terrific James Earl Jones and Brad Dourif) was more compelling than the individual episodes to introduce.

Tales From The Darkside: The Movie (1990) was John Harrison's decent revival of the cheap 'n' cheerful 1980s TV horror series, with a fun Deborah Harry as a homicidal housewife distracted from fattening up a kid for dinner by the stories he tells about a mummy, an indestructible cat and a bargaining gargoyle. *Necronomicon* (1993), linked by the wonderful Jeffrey Combs as an inspiration-seeking H.P. Lovecraft, dispenses with conventional monsters and EC-like moral twists in favor of a stylish combination of Poe-like Gothic romanticism ("The Damned") and mad-science ("The Cold").

Rusty Cundieff's *Tales From The Hood* (1995) was a rare, theatrically released horror anthology during this period, and it is well worth rediscovering. The most successful of a handful of movies in the 1990s that channeled the 1970s blaxploitation cycle, it stars Clarence Williams III as a sinister mortuary keeper foretelling the fates of homeboys he ultimately leads into Hell (a là various Amicus anthologies) and explaining how four corpses came to be. The stories that follow are socially aware tales about the welfare system, police brutality, black crime and slavery. *Rogue Cop Revelation* has black activist Tom Wright returning from the grave to avenge his death at the hands of brutish cops Wings Hauser and Michael Massee, while *Boys Do Get Bruised* is an outstanding story of an abused kid whose violent stepdad is far scarier than the monsters of his fantasies. This episode has the film's best effect, a "crumpled man" visual courtesy of surrealist Screaming Mad George.

KKK Comeuppance, about racist politician Corbin Bernsen getting his just deserts via manikins possessed by executed black slaves, has some first-rate old-school FX (by the Chiodo Brothers), bringing to life a cool new take on *Trilogy of Terror's* Zuni doll segment. And *Hard Core Convent* is a novel spin on *A Clockwork Orange*, in which mass-murderer Lamont Bentley is subjected to a new government rehab program that involves being chained to a table and forced to endure endless images of violence by and against blacks (including scenes from *Boyz n The Hood).*

The only other urban black-themed horror anthology worth a damn is *Snoop Dogg's Hood of Horror* (2006), an uneven but somewhat underrated attempt to fashion the eponymous rapper into a kind of self-promoting, skinny hipster version of the Crypt Keeper. None of the three stories that he frames have any great merit, but

the movie has enough witty ideas and clever gore gags to make it a sound choice for a Friday night rental. The best is the middle segment, about a racist white Texan (Anson Mount) who has sex to the tune of *Cotton Eyed Joe*, has a brain-dead girlfriend ("Do me, Elvis style!") and naturally endures a nasty comeuppance. Although the final story, in which rapper Pooch Hall finds success the wrong way, does feature a very endearing zombie rapper who advises against acceptance speeches at awards ceremonies: "I talked to God. Quit thanking him, he doesn't give a shit…"

The flip-side of the coin from the turn of the century is the equally overlooked *Terror Tract* (2000), a stylish horror satire in which struggling real estate agent John Ritter displays an unusual level of honesty as he takes two prospective buyers around three houses in a spectacularly screwed-up neighborhood, relating tales of vengeful cadavers, rampaging monkeys and a creepy meat-cleaver wielding maniac in an old lady rubber mask whose signature line is "Come to Granny." The movie's trump card is its very end, in which the threats from all three separate stories come together and the suburban street explodes into chaos. Among other horrors, Bobo the monkey mauls a passer-by while a guy calmly runs over his cat with a lawnmower.

Given that the first half of the first decade of the 21st century was dominated by Asian horror, it's no surprise that the horror anthology enjoyed a revival courtesy of Eastern filmmakers. The Pang Brothers gave us *Bangkok Haunted* (2001), a visually assured but over-extended compendium of scary tales related by three women in a café. Typical of the post-*Scream*, post-modern movement in contemporary horror, these characters take on the audience's perspective by pondering over the ambiguities and flaws in each of the stories as they unfold. They even jokingly suggest titles for the second epi-

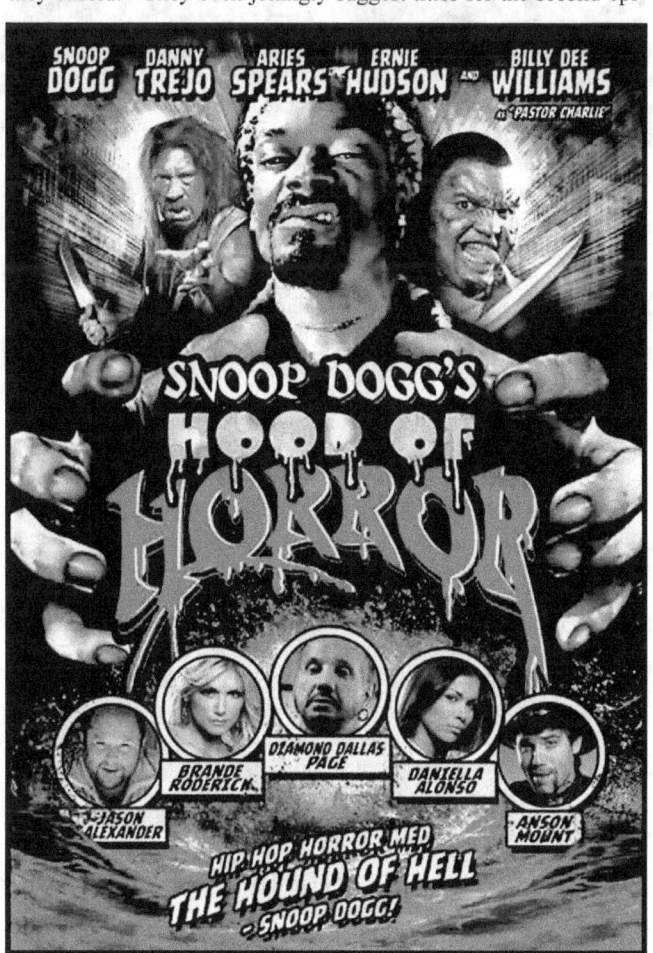

sode, coming up with the to-the-point *Horror Sex on A Horrific Night* and *Put Her In A Grave With Pleasure*.

There's no framing device in either *Three* (2002) or its sequel *Three Extremes* (2003)—just a trilogy of horror stories by three prominent filmmakers. The standout in the former is Kim Jee-Won's *Memories*, a melancholic mind-bender with powerful imagery including an ashen-faced woman who literally picks her brain, severed fingers raining from the ceiling of a dingy bathroom and a dismembered woman turning up in a gym bag. *Three Extremes*, on the other hand, has three very different but equally impressive mini-movies.

The biggest surprise about this one is that Takashi Miike's Japanese entry, *The Box*, contrary to his reputation, is the most restrained—a deliberately paced, David Lynch–influenced mood piece about a haunted novelist unable to shake off her twin-sister's demise. The Hong Kong entry *Dumplings,* by Fruit Chan, is extraordinary in lots of ways and centers around Bai Ling's use of unborn fetuses to make her unique rejuvenating dumplings. Chan busts taboos with style in this rich satire of vanity in which the vain and selfish get their comeuppance. We learn that first-borns are the most nutritious, while those spawned by incest have greater potency (!). Finally, from Korea, Park Chan Wook's *Cut* is a dazzling display of its maker's craft and audacity, with incongruous dance sequences and breathtaking violence punctuating an tense, nervously funny story of a handsome film director held hostage by an underappreciated extra.

Other contributions to the form veered much more toward the formulaic, though *Dark Tales of Japan* (2004), in which a spooky old woman tells scary stories on a bus, has its moments, including the surrealistic *Spiderwoman*, about a supernatural creature with eight legs and a human face who lures drivers to their doom. But the creature is eventually repelled by the word "hornet" repeated aloud.

The British contribution to the subgenre in this period was limited to DVD fare like *Cradle of Fear* (2001), pepped up by extreme gore and the stunt casting of *Cradle of Filth* front man Dani Filth, and Steve Coogan's wonderful TV pastiche *Dr. Terrible's House of Horrible*. But writer Mark Gattis (who had already paid tribute to Amicus in the Christmas episode of his cult series *League of Gentlemen*) brought things full circle with *Crooked House* (2008), originally made for BBC television and styled as the 21st century equivalent of the BBC's much beloved *Ghost Story For Christmas* series aired throughout the 1960s and 1970s.

Gattis casts himself as a gleefully ghoulish museum curator with a malevolent grin and knowing references to genre clichés, as he relates the dark history of Tudor House Geap Manor to schoolteacher Lee Ingleby. Of the three individual stories, *Something Old*, a 1920s tale of an upper-class girl haunted by a terrifying eyeless bride on the night before her wedding, is genuinely spooky and *The Knocker* delivers a lovely homage to *Dead of Night* as Ingelby's own house keeps changing to reflect Geap Manor's ominous interior; this story also has the best scare—a startling reveal of an eyeless ghoul.

There's a strong British interest in *Trapped Ashes* (2005), a union of five very different filmmakers tied together by Joe Dante's framing story. The frame involves tireless "Ultra Studios" tour guide Henry Gibson relating horror stories from his own industry experience, when his tour bus gets trapped on an old movie set. The Brit connection is Ken Russell's episode *The Girl With the Golden Breasts*, in which pretty Rachel Vetri uses a unique clinic to acquire the bigger tits Hollywood demands from its actresses, only to discover that the enhanced bosoms have an insatiable lust for blood. The other story, notably *My Twin The Worm* by John Gaeta, a David Cronenbergian body horror tale, has its moments, but Russell's has the most sex and surreal laughs, including the eminently quotable line, "I want the old me back without these bloodsucking tits!" and a punch line involving the evil boobs sucking blood from a cocktail straw. The final twist is a straight lift from the Amicus cycle.

The dormant Italian horror film made a lukewarm addition to the subgenre with Sergio Stivaletti's *The Three Faces of Terror* (2004), notable only for Lamberto Bava playing himself on the fake set of *Demons 7* in an attempt at satire. *Fear(s) of the Dark* (2007) was an expressionistic, somewhat pretentious animated French portmanteau framed by musings of the nature of fear and dominated by Gothic-hued monochrome stories of woe and weirdness.

Back in the US, three movies plus *The Simpsons'* annual tradition of *Treehouse of Horror* have kept the form alive. *The Signal* (2007) is an apocalyptic techno-paranoia riff on *Kairo* (among others) that takes the unique form of three separate "transmissions" by three directors, each featuring inter-linked characters at different times in the same crisis. The crisis being that a mysterious signal has infected all our 21st century modes of communication, causing psychosis and madness in a similar fashion to Stephen King's novel *Cell*. This impressive indie's strongest, most idiosyncratic suit is its middle story, a self-contained sitcom from Hell called *The Jealousy Monster*, in which an infected housewife kills her husband with a balloon pump but still goes ahead with her New Year's Eve party.

At a similar (low) budget level is John Simpson's *Amusement* (2009), with influences ranging from *Duel* to *Poltergeist* and a 20-minute wrap-up that explains how three initially unrelated stories are linked by its malevolent, giggling villain.

In this age of redundant remakes and feeble sequels, it is a pleasure to consider that some kind of high in the horror anthology format has been reached with a recent movie. Step forward Michael Dougherty's *Trick 'r Treat* (2007), the final film in our survey and as good a way to bow out this potted history as any. Gorgeously shot, scored and directed, it is that rare movie capturing the feel and spirit of a great, scary, *fun* Halloween night. Dougherty is smart enough to not overplay his loving references to genre favorites from his childhood, but his indulgences (including lovingly illustrated comic book titles a là *Creepshow*) just add to the fun.

The circular narrative structure cleverly weaves four over-lapping episodes, unfolding in the same small town, into a cohesive whole. For once, each story is tonally consistent and equally effective. The opening has just one of the movie's casting coups: the always-excellent Dylan Baker neatly riffs on his creepy *Happiness* paternal persona as a warped principal who kills trick or treaters. In the second story, pals of 22-year-old Anna Paquin are desperate for her to lose her cherry, but their party-night mission turns out to be a skin-shredding werewolf initiation rather than a sex-fest, in one of the movie's many moments of imaginative misdirection.

The best scares and creeps come in the final two segments, with a wonderfully atmospheric homage to John Carpenter's *The Fog* as a group of kids invoke the town legend of a school bus massacre and fall victim to the risen dead. This episode in particular revisits that rarely achieved sense of old-school spook house ambience, while the final story begins as a marvelous tribute to *Amelia*, with Brian Cox as a grouchy Halloween-hating loner menaced by a pint-sized, sack-masked ankle-slashing trick or treater. Typical of the movie as a whole, the punch line takes the story somewhere else entirely.

Dougherty bucks 21st century trends for sadism and cheap jolts, making sparing but effective use of gore and having a lot of witty fun with genre archetypes like the virgin, the neighborhood old-timer and the bullied outsider. It's one of the few contemporary genre movies you look forward to seeing again, even while watching it the first time.

Allow us a moment of sentimental reflection. I still nurse fond memories of my parents getting a VCR for the first time back in the mid-1980s, with *Creepshow* being the first movie they ever rented. That film, and scores of other movies, helped shape and develop my burgeoning love of horror movies. *Trick 'r Treat*, destined to be one of the great horror anthologies, should have the same effect on any impressionable, intelligent youngster lucky enough to stumble upon it. And so it continues one generation to the next. Remade for its own generation, classic horror marches onward.

BOOK REVIEW
MIDNIGHT MARQUEE
By Gary J. Svehla

Horror Noir: Where Cinema's Dark Sisters Meet by Paul Meehan; McFarland www.mcfarlandpub.com; Order 800-253-2187; 304 pages soft cover $39.95

I have always been intrigued about the relationship between horror cinema and film noir. It seems children love spooky and fantastical cinema, but after seeing all the great and not-so-great movies for the fifth time, now as adults, we tend to gravitate to the more adult horrors that film noir provides. Paul Meehan draws parallels between classic costume Gothic literature with many woman-in-peril noirs. Meehan reminds us that horror cinema comes in essentially two flavors: supernatural and psychological, and he traces the horror/film noir connection to the mid-1940s when he claims supernatural horror was in retreat (after Universal's *House of Dracula* with the emergence of the Val Lewton RKO factory tapping into the new pulse of horror with his psychological classics). Meehan draws the link between psychological horror and film noir, citing that both deal with the murder pathology of psychotic individuals. He emphasizes the monstrous characters that appear in the cinema of noir, not just monstrous in the psychological sense but also monstrous in size and actions. Meehan points out the short creative distances that exist between horror thrillers such as *Les Diaboliques*, *Psycho* and film noir classics that also focus upon detailed and intelligent crimes carried out by psychologically damaged individuals. Meehan makes the case that both genres emphasize low-key lighting with the absence of fill lights to create a visual world of darkness and shadows. He reminds us that the same creative team that created *Cat People* (1942) also created the similar look and tone in the noir classic *Out of the Past* (1947).

As in similar works where authors try to force their point, Meehan compares Billy Wilder's classic *Sunset Boulevard* to *Dracula*, only with role reversal. In *Sunset Boulevard* the Norma Desmond (Gloria Swanson) character, an aging Hollywood superstar, feeds off the energy and spirit (metaphorically she becomes the vampire feeding off the blood) of young reporter Joe Gillis (William Holden), draining him dry but keeping him happy with materialistic things before killing him off. Meehan refers to Desmond's "Sunset castle" and compares her Gothic servant played by Erich von Stroheim to Dwight Frye's similar character in *Dracula*. By making such comparisons, the book only becomes more interesting. Meehan makes his analogies succinct, and they are always well thought out.

The book includes chapters *Horror Noir in the 1930s; The Val Lewton/Jacques Tourneur Noir Legacy; Horror Noir From Radioland; Monster Noir; Gothic and the Costume Noir; Horror Noir in the 1950s; Hitchcock's Psychological Ghosts and Doppelgangers* and *The Mean Streets of Hell*.

One slight complaint occurs time in and time out. Once the author does an outstanding job of setting up the context of the symbiotic relationship between horror and noir, the writer forgets all this good stuff and simply writes about individual horror movies as though the review could have been lifted from any horror movie book. For instance, the book's cover showcases Fredric March's Mr. Hyde torturing Ivy (Miriam Hopkins) from Paramount's *Dr. Jekyll and Mr. Hyde* (1932), so I reread Meehan's analysis of that horror classic. Meehan spends a paragraph comparing the Robert Louis Stevenson story as being closer to film noir (compared to the more Gothic novels *Frankenstein* and *Dracula*) than other early horror classics, by nature of its psychological focus and mystery setup. He includes analysis of the movie that goes on for several pages, filled with photos as well, and speaks of the directorial style, the performances, the themes, other films that share similar themes, the makeup, synopsis, some examples of stand-out dialogue, etc. But nowhere does Meehan explore this often discussed horror classic as horror *noir* (except perhaps peripherally). The world does not necessarily need another analysis of the Rouben Mamoulian classic, but a review discussing it as horror noir would have been fresh and expected. That aspect never arrived.

But in spite of a few flaws, I really enjoyed this book; I only wished it had maintained the expectations of the early chapters and found that meeting ground between similar genres that share similar tone, themes, photography, musical scores and inherent character types. However, we still have wonderful sections including *Psychoanalyzing The Universal Monsters* that only scratches the surface. The emphasis here is on *Dracula's Daughter* (which contains the beginnings of the femme fatale), *Son of Dracula* (with director Robert Siodmak's film noir recasting of the Dracula/vampire legend), and *The Wolf Man* (which focuses upon the internal psychological struggles of Larry Talbot). The same approach is accorded to the Val Lewton/Jacques Tourneur series of horror thrillers that do contain elements of film noir.

So basically, I enjoyed very much Paul Meehan's approach in illustrating the connections between horror cinema and film noir. He perhaps failed to make the ultimate leap of faith and explore these films with new vision and insight, detailing the noir elements in specific horror films and the horror in specific film noir. But he managed to create an intelligent and highly insightful cross-analysis of both exciting film genres. I recommend the book.

Richard Matheson On Screen: A History of the Filmed Works by Matthew R. Bradley; McFarland www.mcfarlandpub.com; Order 800-253-2187; 305 pages soft cover $45.00

The book opens by listing all the films based upon novels, short stories or original screenplays by author Richard Matheson, one of the true movers and shakers of horror cinema (and of course his contribution to *The Twilight Zone* TV series was essential to the success of that series).

Matthew R. Bradley's insightful introduction lays out the genesis of the long and fruitful career of author Richard Matheson, who was a member of the Southern California gathering of writers sometimes known as "the Group" or, as Robert Bloch referred to them, The Matheson Mafia (Richard Matheson, Ray Bradbury, Robert Bloch, William F. Nolan and Charles Beaumont). In the introduction, Bradley quotes from original research and other published sources to tell the tale.

It is amazing to think that Richard Matheson's first cinematic success was adapting his own novel *The Shrinking Man* to the screen as *The Incredible Shrinking Man*, a Universal science fiction classic directed by Jack Arnold and starring Grant Williams. In many ways, even when we consider the movie was produced as a moderate-budgeted B programmer, *The Incredible Shrinking Man* may be considered a classic of the genre and remains one of Matheson's finest cinematic contributions. It is so rare to be offered an Existentialist probing of man's purpose transformed into a Saturday afternoon matinee programmer, complete with giant cats and a spider.

Bradley does a good job of offering each Matheson movie chronologically. Besides including interview quotes from his own conversations (most already published) with Matheson, Bradley includes telling quotes from other published interview sources. The author covers the production history of each movie and provides an insightful critique, including a brief synopsis that never gets in the way of the merits of the production. And as is expected, Bradley keeps the focus on Matheson, his contribution as a writer, how he concocted the story (or novel) and how he translated the original printed page to the screen. Analysis includes differences between the published novel and the final screenplay as shot. I can say chapters such as the one on *The Incredible Shrinking Man* are close to being definitive analyses. We even have the director's perspective from the book *Inside Jack Arnold*. And what I like most is that Richard Matheson and his contributions always remain front and center.

Of course, moving on to the second chapter and his screenplay for a film called *The Beat Generation*, a film less substantial and important than the classic *The Incredible Shrinking Man*, we of course have fewer published sources to tell the story as thoroughly as was done with the first screenplay. The only quotes from Matheson about his contribution appear in a short 1992 letter to the author where he comments about the film's failure. Bradley shares how another youth-in-revolt screenwriter of the time rewrote portions of the Matheson script to make it more hip.

Of course a classic such as *The Incredible Shrinking Man* deserves more coverage and historical analysis than an exploitative melodrama such as *The Beat Generation* does. However, to play Devil's Advocate for a moment, so much has already been written about the movie classics that perhaps we crave more coverage for the seldom-seen duds. The most important aspect is that Bradley provides some insight from Richard Matheson for each and every movie.

The book shines in the chapter on Richard Matheson's contribution to the classic TV series *The Twilight Zone* because the chapter is primarily composed of Matheson's personal reflections about the episodes he wrote. Of course quotes from published interviews of other creative participants are included as well. From the viewpoint of cinematic history, one could not ask for more. This chapter morphs into a chapter on *Other Episodic Television* where we are exposed

to scripts Matheson wrote for shows such as *Lawman, Wanted Dead or Alive, Thriller, Night Gallery, Ghost Story* and many, many more.

Perhaps one of my favorite Richard Matheson screenplays was the very first Roger Corman–directed Edgar Allan Poe horror classic *House of Usher*, featuring Vincent Price in what was to be his cinematic legacy, starring in a series of movies based upon the writings of Poe. For me the lethargic and atmospheric *House of Usher* remains my favorite of all the series. Of course it was the first contribution by Matheson to American-International Pictures and it began a professional relationship working for James Nicholson and Samuel Z. Arkoff, one that put Matheson's name up in lights in a string of successful movies for the company (not all of them Poe derived). Remember, AIP never depended upon artistic screenwriters before now (they produced films such as *The She-Creature, Earth vs. The Spider* and *How To Make A Monster*). The chapter contains just enough analysis, production detail and published quotes (both from primary and secondary sources) to provide the insights needed. And of course Matheson's contributions are fully illuminated.

True, a book on Richard Matheson is only as interesting as the movies he wrote for the screen and television, but surprisingly, Matheson, with perhaps a few missteps, created an impressive body of work and this book does his legacy more than justice. It is an interesting book for any a fun of science fiction, fantasy and horror cinema.

DVD REVIEW
MIDNIGHT MARQUEE

BY GARY J. SVEHLA

Rating: 4 (excellent); 3 (good);
2 (fair); 1 (poor)

Universal Horror Classic Movie Archive
Movies: *The Black Cat* (2.5);
Man Made Monster (3.0);
Horror Island (2.5); *Night Monster* (3.0);
Captive Wild Woman (2.5); Disc: 3.5
Universal

All the classic Universal horror movies are finally out on DVD only the lost-between-the-cracks B pro;grammers remain, but some of those B productions are minor gems. Specifically, movies such as *Man Made Monster* (which introduced Lon Chaney, Jr. to Universal horror) and the seldom seen *Night Monster* (with an eerie Bela Lugosi) are movies that pack a wallop and haven't been seen with such pristine appearance since their original releases. Let's be upfront. Fans won't find any *Bride of Frankenstein*, *Abbott and Costello Meet Frankenstein* or *The Mummy* here. But for fans of B productions, and specifically of Universal B productions, this box set contains a virtual feast for only $20.

The 1941 *The Black Cat* is not anywhere near Edgar Ulmer's 1934 classic starring Boris Karloff and Bela Lugosi. Interestingly, the film is not even a remake, even though Universal produced the movie and Bela Lugosi plays a lurking character presence as the gardener Eduardo, disguised in heavy makeup. The camera loves to linger on Lugosi hiding outside a window or jump-cutting to a huge close-up of his face. But his performance is a marginal one and serves as a frightening figure to boost suspense and fear. Lugosi looks terrific but does little else except pose for the camera.

The Black Cat has been reborn as an old dark house murder mystery. Old crazy woman Henrietta Winslow (Cecilia Loftus) lives in a rickety mansion overrun with her beloved cats (although she avoids black cats, a symbol of evil). Her vulture-like relatives surround her and kiss her ass, knowing they want to be included in her will, so they do whatever it takes to remain on her good side. Henrietta sees right through them. She fears that such dastardly relatives will contest her will, which leaves her estate to her equally weird housekeeper Abigail Doone (Gale Sondergaard), and provides that Doone will continue to care for her cats. No one will get any money until Doone dies, but Henrietta announces precisely what every relative will net. In spite of her bold actions to avoid a family implosion, the kindly old matriarch is found dead, at first assumed to have accidentally fallen and impaled herself on her long knitting needles. But the audience immediately realizes it's a case of murder.

Brash Broderick Crawford plays a conniving man who wishes to buy Henrietta's house, and his partner is Hugh Herbert, who plays a comical antiques dealer who wants to also buy every piece of furniture in the mansion. Instead of coming off as cruel opportunists, Crawford and Herbert assay the comic relief parts and serve as outsiders who try to solve the mystery involving secret passages and hidden rooms. Even main star Basil Rathbone has practically nothing to do, except take secret phone calls that allude to massive debts that will be paid off very soon. Upcoming star Alan Ladd, looking very short, plays anger and impatience and very little else as one of the heirs-to-be. Besides Crawford and Herbert, the only standout besides Cecilia Loftus is the always-reliable Gale Sondergaard, who was made to haunt old dark houses. Her weirdness helps carry the film, especially in one sequence where the camera pulls tight on her and she simply laughs wildly, almost cackles, as the others draw toward one another in fear.

The mystery is solved as Hugh Herbert pulls a grab bag of tricks out of his jacket, be it little tools or oil or glue, to repair antiques that he comically broke. The horror finally arrives at the film's ending, as the action moves to Henrietta's crematorium for her cats, a crematorium that is also large enough to burn human beings to a crisp. And before one innocent victim is incinerated in the oven, the murderer is revealed and that person is set ablaze. In an effective sequence,ol;pppp the fiend becomes engulfed in fire and runs outside to burn alive. Nothing is

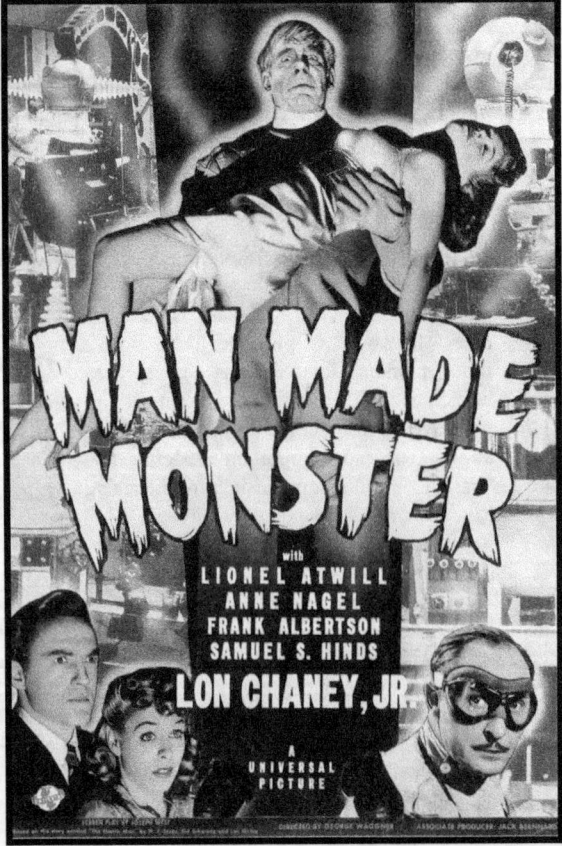

new or original in *The Black Cat*, but for 70 minutes, it does manage to entertain.

Man Made Monster, also released in 1941, becomes the star attraction of the boxed set, featuring Lon Chaney, Jr.'s first starring performance for Universal. Working with iconic mad doctor Lionel Atwill, *Man Made Monster* is one terrific monsterfest lasting a scant 59 minutes.

Lon Chaney, in perhaps his finest horror performance, plays "Dynamo" Dan the Electric Man, a sideshow carnival performer who admits his Electric Man act is mostly phony, although he does absorb large doses of electricity, making him more immune to the juice than the average citizen. When the bus he is hiding on hits an electrical generator, everyone is killed except Dan, and the kindly Dr. Lawrence (Samuel S. Hinds) asks Dan to submit to experiments to discover why he has developed an immunity to large volts of electrical current. When the doctor mentions free meals and board, Dan is all smiles and readily agrees to put his health in the hands of strangers. This affability and folksy kindness establishes Chaney, Jr.'s Dan McCormick as a performance well within his range. Along with Lennie from *Of Mice and Men*, "Dynamo" Dan is the perfect role for Chaney, Jr. because it does not require deep psychological insight (as Chaney, Jr. is required to do as Larry Talbot in *The Wolf Man*). Working within the hour-long B programmer format, Chaney, Jr. has found his niche and submits one of his best roles in one of his best films, period. He was never intended to be dashing romantic leading-man material (his wooing of Evelyn Ankers in *The Wolf Man* is almost ridiculous), so when "Dynamo" Dan seems more attached to the pet dog than Anne Nagel, this seems perfectly natural for his character.

But the horror elements ring strong in *Man Made Monster*. When Dr. Lawrence is called away to a convention and evil assistant Dr. Rigas (Lionel Atwill) takes over the experiments, we know that the mad doc will transform the good-natured Dan into a monster by the third act of the film. And the transformation occurs in subtle ways. First, between treatments, Dan becomes lethargic and physically drained of energy, almost as though his body needs the electrical treatments. By the end of the electrical infusion experiments, "Dynamo" Dan the human being is brain dead and becomes a zombie who feeds off the energy of others. Unless he wears a rubber suit, anything he touches will drain off his life's energy. Now sporting an electrical glow similar to the glow effect in *The Invisible Ray*, Dan's face is sunken in and wrinkled, his deep-set eyes black and lifeless. He has become an energy-feeding monster, the direct opposite to Dan's former personality. However, whether playing the down-home average Dan or the transformed electrical monster, Lon Chaney, Jr. does a fantastic job with his performance. This role, although varied, is not unduly demanding. Chaney, Jr. is allowed to portray type and attitude, and the limited actor rises to the occasion. When Chaney, Jr. played the typical Chaney role, he did a fine job. When directors and screenwriters required him to become another personality type, the actor experienced difficulties. Too bad Hollywood never understood the actor's limitations. Had Chaney, Jr. been allowed to prosper in the B film arena with more stereotyped roles, he would have probably earned higher renown than he suffered at the hands of critics when he attempted roles of greater emotional depth (Larry Talbot in *The Wolf Man*, all his leads in the *Inner Sanctum* mystery series, etc.). But as seen here in his first Universal starring performance, Lon Chaney, Jr. owns the role of Dan McCormick and demonstrates one of his finest performances in an exemplar B horror production.

Apparently 1941 was a stellar year for Universal horror-themed B productions, and the almost forgotten *Horror Island* may be one of the best. Directed by George Waggner the same year he was to direct *The Wolf Man*, *Horror Island* takes the old dark house horror mystery and transforms it into a seafaring (although the ship is docked at the harbor) pirate's treasure buried in a haunted castle scenario. First off, *Horror Island* bears similarities to the earlier discussed *The Black Cat* (1941), but *The Black Cat* plays its threadbare theme by the numbers and does not deviate from the pattern. To disguise the anemic plot, Universal hired some major stars for box-office attraction—Basil Rathbone, Bela Lugosi, Hugh Herbert, Brod Crawford and Gale Sondergaard—but failed to use them as anything more than window dressing. *Horror Island*, on the other hand, has an entirely B movie cast but does far more with the overall performances and production. Take the starring team of Bill Martin (Dick Foran) and Tobias Clump (Leo Carrillo). In *Horror Island* Martin is the former university professor who decides to chuck his high-pressure life and buy a boat and live a life of adventure. Martin is always one step ahead of bill collectors and never takes life too seriously. Along for the comic relief angle is Clump, a peg-legged seaman who has half of his pirate's treasure map, the other half stolen, and now working with Martin, the duo hopes to recover the missing

map piece and find the treasure. As though one comic relief character wasn't enough, Martin's friend Stuff (played by Fuzzy Knight, best known as a B Western sidekick) acts dutifully frightened but remains true blue. Yes, this is a boys' fantasy and the leads are those lazy yet noble men that kids admire.

Horror Island shines almost from the first frame where the camera follows the peg leg of Clump as he lurks at harbor storefronts trying to find the one that belongs to Bill Martin. A policeman, suspicious, intervenes and directs the pirate-dressed Clump to Martin's boat. However, in the shadows lurks The Phantom (Foy Van Dolsen), the almost comic-book Shadow-esque villain, the man who will soon jump Clump and steal half of his pirate's map. The sequences with The Phantom are well lit, or should I say lit to shadowy perfection. These early sequences aboard the Skiddoo feature the three seafarers planning to recover the missing map. Unknown to them The Phantom boards the ship and listens in, such moody sequences increasing the scare quotient.

Then the action moves on to *Horror Island*, and of course The Phantom also follows the now expanded crew of seafarers and professors and damsels in distress. In the best tradition of Agatha Christie, the fiend (is it The Phantom or not?) leaves signs listing the number of people left alive, as victims begin to fall left and right. In fact one of the chief flaws of *Horror Island* is that as the body count climbs, little suspense is used to accentuate the demise of each victim. A victim might be wearing armor and simply falls over to be discovered inside the armor dead. For instance, The Phantom dies unexpectedly as he hides behind cover and the real villain uses a crossbow to pierce his heart quickly and silently. Even the villain, of course the most surprising and least likely person, dies quickly and with too little fanfare. However, the haunted corridors of the castle with swinging battle weapons hanging over doors create a haunted house menagerie of thrills and chills, and these sequences are handled much more creatively than similar sequences in *The Black Cat* (1941). Simply put, *Horror Island* lacks the star power of *The Black Cat*, but *Horror Island* contains the better characters, better plotting and better direction. And Elwood Bredell's cinematography shines, making this one of the best-filmed B Universals ever.

Night Monster has the best reputation of all the old dark house mysteries in this set. It definitely trumps *The Black Cat* and features the star power (Bela Lugosi and Lionel Atwill) lacking in *Horror Island*. But taking the best of both cinematic worlds, *Night Monster* features the star power along with the quirky plot and moody photography in a B film rich with haunted mansion set design. To be honest, it lacks the scope of *Horror Island* but does manage to chill the blood in several spooky sequences. And fortunately, the film's ridiculous plot moves rapidly forward under the capable hands of serial director Ford Beebe.

The film begins in classic Universal horror style as pretty Milly the maid

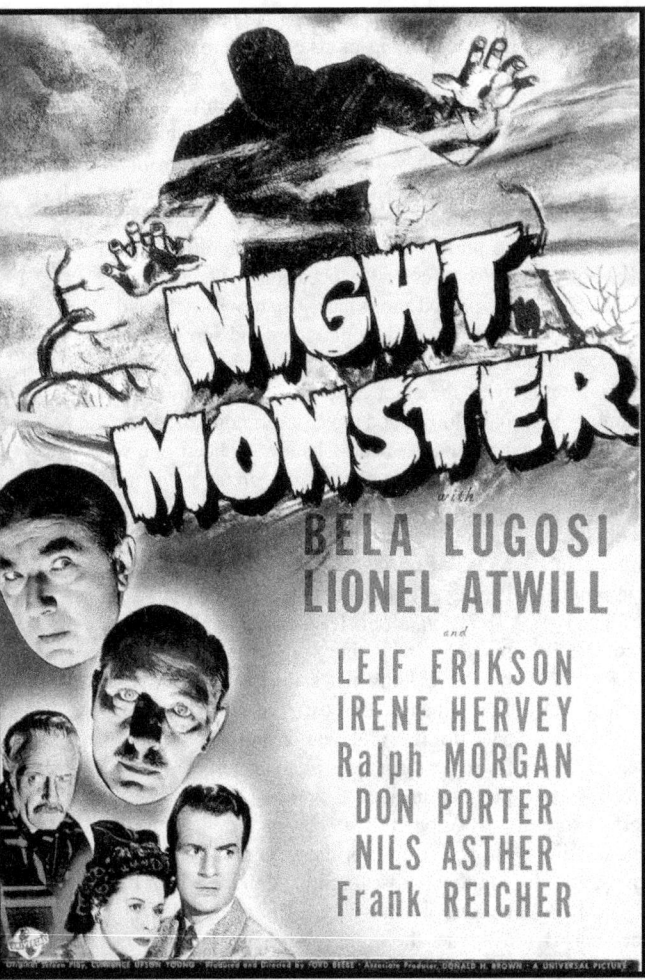

announces things have grown too strange around the mansion, so she is quitting. A driver waits for her just outside the gated entrance to the estate, but he leaves before she arrives, hearing a voice announce that she changed her mind and would be staying. After the driver leaves, Milly appears at the gate with her suitcase and is forced to venture forth alone in the fog with the croaking frogs providing the tense soundtrack. Legend states when the frogs stop croaking, the marsh fiend will strike. At this exact moment, the frogs stop making noise (in an almost silly effect that makes it appear that some sound technician simply turned off the frog sound effects switch) and the figure of the marsh phantom soon confronts Milly, whose screams are heard by a visiting psychiatrist, Dr. Harper (Irene Hervey), whose car has broken down beyond the mansion gates. Within the next day or so, Milly is found in a pool of water strangled and dead. What a fantastic way to start the proceedings in classic Universal style.

The story involves elderly Kurt Ingston (Ralph Morgan), maimed and disfigured by a team of doctors who actually saved his life. The crippled and shriveled elderly man is bedridden and spends part of his day in a wheel chair, hardly able to get about. Prosthetics have replaced his two actual arms, and one leg has been amputated above the knee, the other one slightly below. Kurt's sister Margaret is a troubled woman who needs psychological help (thus the arrival of Dr. Harper), mostly caused by the dark family secret she harbors. Also arriving are the three doctors who disfigured Ingston, with the grateful old man inviting them to the house to thank them for all they tried to do for him. But of course, within a short period of time the doctors (and other household victims) begin turning up dead, unfortunately, the underused Lionel Atwill being among the first. But even Laurie (a youthful Leif Erickson) the chauffeur is found hanging dead in a bedroom closet. Bela Lugosi, who plays chief servant and house butler Rolf, gets to say and do more than he did in his window dressing role in *The Black Cat*, but Lugosi is once again woefully underused. The gaunt Lugosi does have the opportunity to bellow commands and look stern, but his major action involves walking up and down the staircase.

Even though once the body count begins suspense is generally lacking in the execution of the murders, the photography by Charles Van Enger rises to the occasion. In one sequence the doctor awaits the arrival of the butler, who will knock on his bedroom door in a special rhythmic pattern. When the knock occurs, the doctor opens his door and we experience a p.o.v. shot from the killer's eyes as the terrified doctor reacts, backing up with horror in his eyes. In another wonderful death sequence, a second doctor sits in the dark at his desk as the stiff shadow of a giant, lumbering figure appears on his wall. The doctor turns around and sees the fiend rushing the camera until the screen turns dark, his gasping scream bellowing. In another odd sequence, mentalist Agor Singh (Nils Asther) performs a parlor illusion where he goes deep into a trance and materializes a human skeleton that extends its arms forward as if to present a jewelry box. However, beneath the box, his palms drip blood. And even after the mentalist is awakened from his trance and the skeleton vanishes, the blood on the carpet remains. This is one of many odd sequences from *Night Monster*.

Finally after everyone figures out that Ingston has been using the mental powers learned from Singh to create artificial limps and arms to be able to get around, the climax occurs in the dense fog surrounding the estate. Ingston, with his arms extended outward in Glenn Strange Frankenstein Monster manner, lumbers upon artificial legs that he is only now learning how to use. Still he is able to gain speed on his young and healthy victims—hero Don Porter and lovely Dr. Harper—as his ultra-human strength and gleeful monstrous eyes give him the distinct advantage. However, a gunshot from afar strikes the deathblow, as sister Margaret torches the house that soon becomes an inferno. Of course we should not be shocked to learn that Ingston invited the doctors to his house to carry out his twisted plan of revenge by ritualistically murdering them. Others, such as Milly, observed the fully restored Ingston walking through the bog and, unfortunately, had to be silenced before the secret got out.

Night Monster becomes a low-rent variation of the synthetic flesh idea from *Doctor X*, but as recreated in this low-rent scenario the effect is oddly off-putting yet slightly silly, even if well photographed in densely foggy marsh settings. *Night Monster* earns points for being audacious if not always believable.

Finally, 1943's *Captive Wild Woman* concludes the box set. Along with *Man Made Monster*, *Captive Wild Woman* may well be the other best movie in the set and entertains because of its cross-genre action approach. Upcoming B director Edward Dmytryk directs and his audacious style, combining wild animal circus action with mad scientist human-to-animal glandular hi-jinks, produces 61 minutes of horrific thrills. It does not hurt to have John Carradine heading up the cast as Dr. Sigmund Walters, the misguided doctor who believes it is acceptable to sacrifice human lives in the name of scientific advancement. Once again Evelyn Ankers plays the leading lady, Beth, whose ill sister (Martha MacVicar) is under the treatment of Dr. Walters for a glandular disorder. Oddly, Milburn Stone portrays the dashing leading man, a wild animal trainer who is not afraid to step inside a cage with ferocious lions and tigers poised to rip him apart. Not the obvious choice to play such a role, his casting was based mostly on his physical similarity to Clyde Beatty, whose actual wild animal taming stock footage becomes the dramatic impetus for the entire film. If we look closely, it is easy to see that Beatty is not Stone, and vice versa, but when caught up in all the action, the two actors blend seamlessly into one.

And non-actor Acquanetta makes her screen debut here, the beauty from Burma, her exotic features making her appear as though she could be an actual evolution of ape into woman. While Acquanetta does not deliver many lines, she is required to react facially in close-up and that she does with poise and enthusiasm. Say what you may, Acquanetta was not hired for her thespic talents but for her looks (and stunt work in makeup as the regressed ape woman). For what she is required to do, Acquanetta does a more than credible job as Paula the Ape Woman, and her otherworldly persona suits the film perfectly.

John Carradine is at his best in his small operating room speaking to his nurse as she chastises him for daring to sacrifice the lives of innocent victims for his work, and with a glimmer in his eye, at this precise moment, realizes that her brain would be perfect for his glandular operation, sacrificing her for the cause of science (and also shutting her up for good). Carradine, almost looking dashing and handsome in a smarmy way, becomes the archetype mad scientist and submits one of his best B performances.

Perhaps the film achieves its B classic status when Fred Mason (Stone), who is dependent upon the piercing eyes of Paula to control the wild animals when he is in the cage with them, canoodles with the real woman of his desires, Beth, making Paula insanely jealous. After witnessing the lovey-dovey exchange between the two, Paula returns to her dressing room and tears it apart in anger. She believed falsely that Fred loved her, but now her heart is broken and her anger ignited. Such an emotional rage regresses the glandular operation that Dr. Walters performed, turning Paula from her beautiful exotic self into a were-ape, a female ape with furry hands and claws and a simian face. Dr. Walters has to sacrifice yet another human to return Paula to fully human status, and that sacrifice of course happens to be Dorothy, sister of Beth. A wild climax results with the caged ape getting loose and causing havoc in the lab, with the good guys coming out on top.

Captive Wild Woman is generally given short shrift, with Acquanetta becoming the Universal whipping girl, second only to Rondo Hatton as Universal horror's worse performer. However, Acquanetta does exactly what is required of her performance and does it effectively. Too bad Universal

did not release all three Ape Woman movies as a box set, because when scrutinized with these gorgeous prints, the entire trilogy becomes even more effective as a B series worth watching.

Given these five remastered movies only cost $20 with beautiful packaging, fans should not moan that no extras exist. For me, the movie's the thing ... the only thing that matters. And this Universal B horror collection is well worth revisiting.

The Boris Karloff Collection
Movies: *Night Key* (2.5);
Tower of London (3.0); *The Climax* (2.0);
The Strange Door (2.0);
The Black Castle (2.0); Disc: 3.5
Universal

Poor Boris!

A few years ago Universal released something they labeled *The Bela Lugosi Collection*, with all but one movie featuring Boris Karloff as sometimes the major star, appearing along with Bela Lugosi. *Murders in the Rue Morgue* starred Lugosi solo. But *The Raven* featured Karloff in a pivotal supporting role. Both icons were equally billed in *The Black Cat*. But Karloff was the dominant star in *The Invisible Ray* and

Black Friday. Why wasn't the boxed-set (containing only one disc no less) called *The Karloff-Lugosi Collection*? Here is the reason ... Universal can now release the remaining (and often inferior) Karloff titles in the aptly titled *The Boris Karloff Collection*. But when compared to the Lugosi set, the Karloff collection pales.

One of the surprises is the first-time-to-home-video release of the crime drama *Night Key*, a movie where Karloff plays sympathetic old age to perfection. Karloff's David Mallory lives in a low-rent brownstone with his beautiful young daughter Joan (Jean Rogers). Mallory is the victim of a nasty Samuel Hines, who stole Mallory's patent and made a fortune from Mallory's state-of-the-art burglary alarm system (as revenge for the love of his life marrying Mallory instead of him!). Mallory has been working feverishly for 15 years to create an upgrade that he wants to sell to Hines to provide an easier life for his daughter, and Hines signs the contract, but he cheats Mallory once again by buying the product but not bringing it to market ... and Mallory does not get more than $500 until the product is marketed. Mallory, savvier this time, decides to destroy what he created by using his new electro-gizmo to turn the burglary system off at major stores, demonstrating the disaster that he can cause if Ranger does not utilize his upgraded product now. Soon the criminal element becomes involved and kidnaps Mallory to allow them to pull off crimes effortlessly.

Night Key demonstrates a different kind of Karloff character, a loving father, a spurned inventor and a clever artist of revenge ... but he never crosses over into insanity or perversity, as did Janos Ruhk. With his failing eyesight (racing against time to finish his invention before going totally blind) resulting in a marvelous panic sequence in the middle of a busy street after his glasses are smashed as he crosses, Karloff's character wins our sympathy as the man is repeatedly victimized. As he slowly gains his revenge by demonstrating his ability to undermine security systems at expensive product stores, he leaves a note signed "Night Key" as a calling card, forcing his hand in this wily game of intimidation. However, the movie is never more than a solid B programmer and demonstrates the type of movie Universal was forced to concoct during the infamous horror ban in the late 1930s.

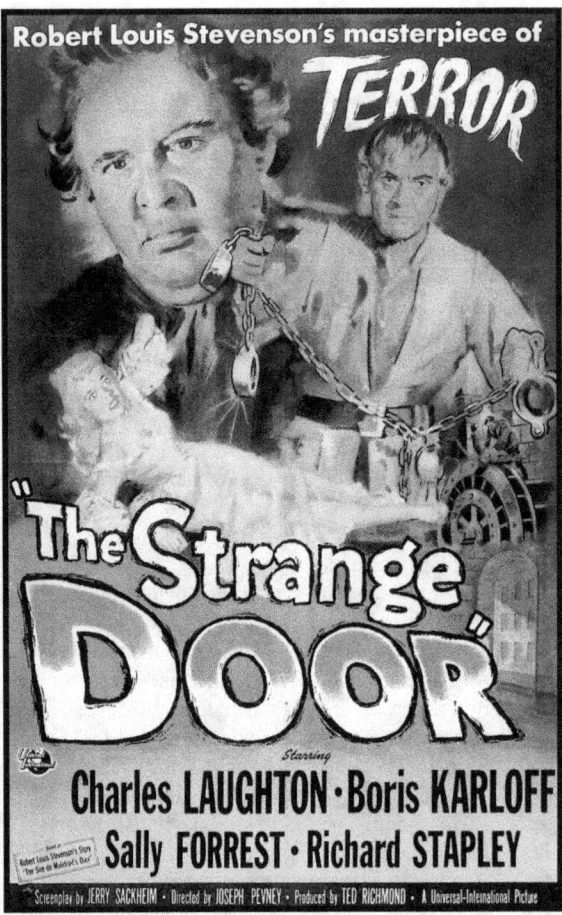

Tower of London is also a non-horror movie. It is a straight historic costume drama produced and directed by Rowland V. Lee, the man responsible for *Son of Frankenstein*, also made in 1939. Karloff, billed second to Basil Rathbone, plays a beefed up supporting role as executioner Mord, a club-footed "hit man" for ruthless Richard, who tries to win the English throne, being 6th in the line of succession. Karloff, bald with black bushy eyebrows, towers above the cast with his Frankenstein monster–style boots and elongated legs, emphasized by his dark tights. His one execution of a patriot is exceptional, with the doomed-to-die man offering the lowest payment possible as a bribe to cut off the head with one skilled strike of the axe. Karloff spits in the hand that received the money and throws the coin away, as the victim is lowered onto the chopping block and Mord cocks back his giant metallic axe and strikes.

But this is Rathbone's movie, and his miniature-model royal throne room houses all those people he has to murder in order to reach the throne. Chilling scenes erupt when another blueblood dies and the chess-like piece is removed from the doll house, as Rathbone gets one step closer to the throne. Of course, Universal did not have the massive sets or money that studios such as Fox or MGM had, so this spectacle period piece seems low-rent by comparison. Especially the battle sequences that seem truncated and bathed in fog. Even Rathbone's masterful swordplay is photographed blandly and he dies with minimal dramatic flair. Mord's death, rolling down the side of the cliff, is much better handled, but he is a supporting player here and Rathbone is the star. Vincent Price, at his most prissy, has a dynamic sequence with Rathbone during a wine-drinking contest that Price thinks he has won when Richard (Rathbone) falls unconscious on the wine-soaked table. However, Clarence (Price) falls into a stupor while Richard awakens, enlisting Mord to help him throw Clarence into a vat of his favorite wine and slamming the wooden top shut, thus drowning the unconscious Clarence and stepping that much closer to the throne.

Tower of London is never better than mediocre but does feature the largest cast of Universal studio supporting players yet assembled (Nan Grey, Leo G. Carroll, Miles Mander, Ian Hunter, Lionel Belmore, Rose Hobart, John Sutton, Donnie Dunagan, Harry Cordon). The characters created by Rathbone, Price and Karloff are of prime interest even if Universal fails to pull off the period details and battle sequences effectively. Big budgeted (for Universal) and ultimately vacuous, *Tower of London* is interesting if lesser Karloff.

People always seem to come down harshly on the two 1950s Universal Gothics. First up is *The Strange Door*, and while the film is slow paced, it does feature some wonderful black-and-white photography by Irving Glassberg, and the art direction (by Bernard Herzbrun, Eric Orborn) and set decoration (by Russell A. Gausman, Julia Heron) are superior. This is one of those black-and-white DVDs so sharp and pristine that the images appear to shimmer. The film's video presentation is simply gorgeous. Based upon a story by Robert Louis Stevenson, no one will ever mistake *The Strange Door* for the superior Val Lewton production of *The Body Snatcher*, but both films seem to thrive on a haunting mood of perversity and a dominant–willed villain.

Unfortunately, Boris Karloff as the manservant Voltan is not that strong-willed villain. That honor goes to Charles Laughton as Alain, who chews up the scenery delightfully. Laughton probably needed the money at the time, and while this

B production is woefully minor for an actor of Laughton's status, he nonetheless has a bunch of ham-fisted fun making his villain shine.

The plot is a simple revenge tale. Denis de Beaulieu (Richard Stapley) is a noble rogue in the Errol Flynn mode. He is handsome, dashing, but irresponsible and caddish, a man who drinks too much, flirts too readily and shoots his pistol one time too many. After being watched and studied by Alain's staff, Denis is lured to Alain's Gothic abode and enters the front door that is unlocked (strangely?). But once inside, Denis finds no handle or latch exits to exit. So like roaches entering the roach motel, it's easy to enter but difficult to get out. Alain plans to keep Denis a happy prisoner … everything he needs will be given him, as long as he marries his niece, the young and beautiful Blanche (Sally Forrest). Alain thinks Denis' social irresponsibility will make their marriage a living hell, but of course the young duo falls in love and Denis is transformed. In his low-key madness, Alain plans to torture the innocent Blanche because her mother is dead and she cannot be punished for breaking his heart, but Alain can punish her daughter. Not quite logical, but Alain's madness is exactly that.

Unknown to Blanche, Alain has kept his brother Edmond (Paul Cavanagh) locked away in a dungeon, leaving the object of his hatred alive only because Edmond appears to also be mad. But in reality, he is very sane and knows he must pretend to scream and rant to remain alive. The mostly unseen Voltan (Karloff) protects Edmond, Denis and Blanche, but by the movie's climax, all three victims are trapped in the dungeon cell with the walls closing in, controlled by a mill water wheel that turns and forces the walls to close in and crush anyone within. However, when Alain falls into the surging waters below, his body momentarily blocks the wheel so the walls stop closing in, but soon his body is crushed and the wheels and gears begin grinding again. Only the fallen and mortally wounded Voltan, who has the key, can save the three, but he lies on the ground near death and rescue is only inches away. This final sequence is the only significant one that Boris Karloff delivers, so his is mostly a supporting role. It's Laughton's show all the way, and the effete and rotund villain is a delight.

The Strange Door is period costume drama of the most Gothic sort, and Universal's small budget gets by because of the already-maintained sets that existed on the back lot that add a feel of superior budgeting. The movie is slow-paced, but

its Gothic mood and major performances get audiences involved. For a minor programmer, *The Strange Door* is oddly interesting and has enough merit to entertain.

Similar in style to *The Strange Door*, *The Black Castle* features the Gothic set decoration that Universal does so well, again employing standing sets from past productions. Once again the cinematography by Irving Glassberg stresses the simmering blacks, grays and whites. The set decoration and art direction by Oliver Emert, Russell A. Gausman, Bernard Herzbrun and Alfred Sweeney create a period detail that foreshadows the costume horror dramas of Hammer Film Productions (although rendered in black-and-white). Produced by Universal ace William Alland and directed by the B master Nathan Juran, the film is once again crippled by a script that fails to utilize the talents of major horror stars such as Boris Karloff and Lon Chaney, Jr. Karloff plays Dr. Meissen, a flunky of evil Count Karl von Bruno (in a delightful performance by Stephen McNally that exudes evil), and it is Meissen's troubled conscience that allows him to save the lives of our hero and heroine, by the movie's end, but sacrifice his own life in the process. Once again Karloff's is a supporting performance, a rather small part for the billing, yet he does a fine job with very little. Lon Chaney, Jr. gets even less screen time, playing a mute animalistic servant who again does the dirty work of the Count, but he does very little in the picture.

As mentioned, Stephen McNally rivals the acting chops of Charles Laughton from *The Strange Door* as main villain, and it is a pity McNally never appeared regularly in the horror film genre, as he is quite excellent in his villainy. Richard Greene, soon to be Robin Hood on British and American television, shines as the avenging angel hero, the man who wants to see the Count dead for the murder of his two close friends. However, his avenging plans are partially waylaid by his romantic interlude with the Count's wife (Rita Corday) and then the Count's jealousy intensifies when he learns that Richard Beckett (Greene) is indeed making a play for his wife (more a trophy wife that he truly does not love … he merely pocesses).

The best part of the movie is its frame. The film begins very similar to *House of Usher* as Beckett and the Countess are apparently lying dead in their coffins, immobile, while voice-over narration from Beckett screams out that he is alive. Of course by the final reel we see how Dr. Meissen used his magic powders to make the duo appear dead so they could be carried out of the castle and later revived. But the sneaky Count knows all and plans to have his adversaries buried alive before they can revive.

The Black Castle attempts to combine romantic adventure and costume horror to produce a hybrid of what Universal did to better effect with the 1939 *Tower of London* and what Hammer would begin a few short years later with *Curse of Frankenstein* and *Horror of Dracula*. But working with a meager budget and journeyman director, *The Black Castle* was doomed to mediocrity, and Universal turned away from Gothic horror and turned to atomic mutation and science gone wild.

This box set seems underwhelming after the more classically stuffed collections that preceded it, such as *The Bela Lugosi Collection*. However, these less seen B productions look terrific re-mastered on DVD and deserve another look and re-evaluation.

**Icons of Horror:
The Sam Katzman Collection**
Movies:
Creature With the Atom Brain (2.5);
The Werewolf (3.0);
The Giant Claw (3.0);
Zombies of Mora Tau (2.5); Disc: 3.5
TriStar/Columbia

He was known as "Jungle Sam" in some circles for producing so many jungle adventures and serials, but the generally disparaged producer of Columbia's B unit, Sam Katzman, is due for re-evaluation. When I was a child the name Katzman, like Ed Wood, was synonymous with grade-Z productions, and it was fashionable to trash any Katzman production. But now seen in hindsight, these collected horror productions (lacking only perhaps *The Man Who Turned to Stone*, which is available separately as a MOD release) are iconic and quite entertaining. A generation ago if anyone mentioned that the horror/science fiction productions of Sam Katzman would be issued in a box set under "the icons of horror" moniker, that person would be laughed out of the room.

Working for Columbia in the mid-1950s and using his Clover Productions banner, Sam Katzman masterminded the profitable B horror bandwagon, and these four productions demonstrate the surprisingly effective results. First up is *Creature With the Atom Brain*, released in 1955, written by Universal ace screenwriter Curt Siodmak and directed by gifted B director Edward L. Cahn. The movie crosses the crime/detective and science fiction genre with very interesting results. Katzman's B horror products always start out fast and finish equally as fast, often with an actor muttering the final line of dialogue as the end title flashes onscreen. Here, the movie begins as a criminal mastermind forces a German scientist to use his atomic brain operation device to create an army of mindless zombies, ready to do his bidding. And in the first sequence a zombie robs and murders his former gangster partner as the victim counts his money and places it in his vault. Crashing through the iron bars and speaking the words of the criminal mastermind Buchanan via microphone, the zombie mutters to his criminal rival he promised he would watch him die, and die he does. The zombie in silhouette lifts the gangster over his head and snaps both his neck and spine in one quick jerk.

It seems that mastermind Buchanan was the mobster who controlled the entire area, but his underlings got greedy and attempted to overthrow the mob boss, who was convicted and deported to Europe, where the current mobsters believe him to be. But working in his underground lead-enforced laboratory, hidden in a typical suburban neighbor home, the mobster murders victims and steals bodies from the morgue to have his accomplice, the German scientist, saw their heads in half and attach atomic controlled metal electrodes to their brains to re-animate them as mindless automatons. Once re-animated, the zombies have super-human strength and only follow the directions given them by Buchanan, who watches everything via a huge TV screen that registers everything the zombies see.

The story gets its bite through the relationship of the two police detectives, Dr. Walker (Richard Denning in his plastered high-hair and pipe-smoking persona) and Captain Dave Harris (S. John Launer), who seem to be modeled on the Jack Webb and Dave Alexander characters from TV's *Dragnet*. Even Walker's cute little girl Penny (Linda Bennett) calls his partner "Uncle Dave" and Dave, unmarried, seems to be a member of the family, often making wife Joyce (Angela Stevens) jealous. Of course the plot develops to the point that poor Uncle Dave is kidnapped and killed by the zombies and is reborn as one. His first task, under Buchanan's direction, is to go to Walker's home to get information (Dave's hat does not hide the scars across his forehead very well; his monotone short bursts of speech should tip the Walkers that something is wrong with Uncle Dave), but the Walkers do not suspect Dave has changed. In a dramatic sequence, once Dave gets the information about the police hiding two members of Buchanan's old gang at headquarters, he abruptly leaves, his calling card being the shattered remains of Penny's beloved doll. Even as a zombie, Uncle Dave leads Walker to the secret laboratory of Buchanan's and helps Walker save the day. However, as the atomic zombies exit the house and assemble on the front lawns, not even grenades from the police can knock them down, and only by turning off the power supply deep in the lab's cellar can the zombies be returned to their formerly dead state.

Creature with the Atom Brain is low budget, of course, yet intriguing. We have interesting family relationships combined with brain-scarred zombies who are running amok, mostly against the criminal underworld. Yet we have a vengeful former mob boss, microphone in hand, glaring into his futuristic videoscope, barking out orders to his zombie army as his powerless German accomplice stands by complaining in the shadows. We have mad labs, zombies, criminals, broken corpses, broken baby dolls and poor Uncle Dave killed after he is

established as a sympathetic character. The movie is nicely paced and well scripted, and the cross genre focus is always interesting.

Next up in 1956's Sam Katzman classic, *The Werewolf*, a film woefully ignored for too long on the home video market (although a shortened super 8mm version was released back in the late 1960s). This film is one of the true B gems of the 1950s, and under the direction of Fred F. Sears, becomes an emotionally involving experience. Most of the kudos for the success of the production must go to relatively unknown star Steven Ritch, who plays the car accident victim who is turned into a werewolf by two unsympathetic doctors who feel the radiation released from nuclear explosions will soon transform the entire human race into monsters. Ritch, playing husband and father Duncan Marsh, loses his memory and wanders into northern California mountain/lake Western-style town (the entire movie was actually filmed on location) trying to understand who and what he is. Ritch's face always registers pain, confusion and terror. He is a family man, a salesman, who only wishes to return home, yet he remembers enough of his werewolf escapades that he does not wish to endanger his family, so he hides out in the snow-covered woods. To create the modern day Western flavor, we have B Western star Harry Lauter playing the deputy to Don Megowan's sheriff (Megowan played the humanized, land based Creature in *The Creature Walks Among Us* and played the Frankenstein Monster in Hammer's TV pilot *Tales of Frankenstein*). These lawman are knuckleheaded boobs who rigidly follow the letter of the law and reluctantly claim we cannot save everyone. Sympathy comes from the elderly town doctor (Ken Christy) and his niece nurse (Joyce Holden), who plead for sympathy and mercy for Marsh when the sheriff and his crew seem to only wish to hunt the man/beast down and kill him.

Wonderful horror sequences abound. In one the evil duo of scientists catch up to the cowering Marsh, who is hiding in a cave. However, when under pressure or stress, Marsh turns into the werewolf, which he does in marvelous time-lapse photography, ending up drooling from his lower mouth as he pounces upon the doctor. The werewolf makeup is very similar to the Andreas makeup from Columbia's *Return of the Vampire* over a decade earlier. Later, we have another wonderful sequence when the werewolf, searching for food, carelessly steps into a trap and struggles to escape, limping away and gaining audience sympathy. In fact, in Marsh's original appearance in town, he is robbed as he leaves a bar late at night and we feel sorry for the hapless victim. As Marsh is backed into a dark alley to be robbed of his last $20, two humans struggle as Marsh turns into the wolf, but this transformation is unseen by the audience. As the werewolf wins the struggle and exits from the alley, an old white-haired woman screams as the audience views the werewolf from the rear, but only in shadows. The film's dual climactic sequences are both gems. In the first, our two evil docs break into the jail to kidnap Marsh to experiment on him, but little do they know that he is faking sleep … as the werewolf. In a wonderfully photographed sequence, the distorted shadows of the jail's bars are projected on the back wall as the werewolf flings the two humans across the cell, making them appear more as rag dolls than human beings. And of course, once the doctors are dead, Marsh escapes. This leads to the final pursuit of the werewolf, with the sheriff and his posse carrying torches that they fling at the hapless wolf. Soon cornering the werewolf who crosses a stone ledge alongside the roadside bridge that overlooks the lake, the sheriff's men wait for Marsh to cross over and then open fire, shooting the sitting duck in the shoulder and gut, killing the man who turns back into human form in death.

The Werewolf shines because of its odd-for-the-time mountain location shooting (featuring dedicated Steven Ritch running barefoot in actual snow), its wonderful cast of characters, its moodily conceived werewolf encounters and the terrific performance by Steven Ritch, who delivers one of the impressive horror performances of the decade. *The Werewolf* is ready for fresh eyes and re-discovery.

One year later, in 1957, director Fred F. Sears and Katzman reunited for the much-aligned *The Giant Claw*, Katzman's attempt to prove that he could produce giant prehistoric monsters without the participation of Ray Harryhausen (with whom he made *It Came From Beneath The Sea*). The truth be told, *The Giant Claw* is one of the best scripted and casted examples of this subgenre; however, Ray Harryhausen's special effects are woefully missed. While Harryhausen fans are quick to trash *The Giant Claw* for its puppet chicken-hawk-from-Hell prehistoric bird, it must be remembered the funky marionette monster does have its charm. Perhaps it's suspension of disbelief, but on the big screen the bird looks pretty horrifying. I think of the sequence where the plane is destroyed and several members parachute below, but one by one, the bird pursues and catches two victims in its wide-open mouth, the humans screaming all the way. For me this sequence works. The oddity of seeing this giant bird monster swooping across the sky, either attacking or being pursued, is frightening. Such sequences do not elicit laughter any longer; they simply amaze me for their audacity.

Add to the mix the participation of stellar sci-fi star Jeff Morrow (as the eccentric Mitch MacAfee) and lovely Mara Corday as his partner in saving the world. Morrow is at first scoffed at when reporting the sighting of the UFO, but once other pilots report the same sightings (sightings not able to be tracked on radar), the generals start to believe. So the film's beginning, besides establishing rugged and well-dimensioned lead characters, tends to play up the mystery of what is this thing in the skies. The bird literally appears as a blur for the longest time until the puppet is at last revealed. Sears paces the film effectively and does not allow the action of the second half to outpace the mystery and suspense of the first. I maintain if the film contained Harryhausen stop-motion, it would be considered a far better film than *It Came From Beneath the Sea*, a dull, talky film too long over-praised. Even with the funky bird, I prefer *The Giant Claw* any day to *It Came From Beneath the Sea*. Sequences of the bird atop the Empire State Building, its wings spread wide, are of course to remind us of a far superior film, but again the audacity of attempting such a

sequence wins my applause for sheer guts alone. For juvenile action and fun, *The Giant Claw* cannot be beat.

Finally this set closes with the under-achiever, *Zombies of Mora Tau*, the least interesting movie in the set. Still, the movie has some interest and in many ways seems to be a low-rent re-thinking of Val Lewton movies such as *Isle of the Dead* and *I Walked With a Zombie*. We have the African coast plantation setting populated by an old woman, in this case Mrs. Peters (Marjorie Eaton), whose husband is among the crew of 10 zombies who protect a sunken ship that attempted to transport diamonds from the area at the turn of the last century. Greed and thievery keep the zombie crew busy, and for them to find eternal peace the diamonds must be returned to the sea forever. Released in 1957 and again directed by Edward L. Cahn, the zombies seem to be more than a tad inspired by Cahn's vision of atomic zombies from *Creature With the Atom Brain*. The bearded seafaring zombies here are again mindless, super strong, unemotional and devoted to killing anyone who approaches the diamonds in the sunken ship.

The cast includes the sleazily stereotyped Allison Hayes as the wife of the project sponsor George Harrison (Joel Ashley). She desires the diamonds to allow her to live the lifestyle she desires, and her husband is all for keeping his sexpot wife happy. Even after Mona has been murdered by the zombies, revived, and returned to Mrs. Peters' house, George cannot accept the obvious fact that his wife is dead. She is cold as ice, does not breathe, has dead eyes and is totally non-communicative. But George thinks a little rest will fix her right up. Mrs. Peters knows the truth, shouts it at George repeatedly, and then surrounds her bed with burning candles, the only thing that frightens the zombies.

The film's best sequences are the staged undersea ones, where leading man Jeff Clark (Gregg Palmer) dons a heavy diving suit and goes underwater to find the diamonds in the sunken ship's safe. George, also underwater, stands guard with a welder's torch in hand, but charging zombies walk on the ocean bottom in the same lethargic manner that they walk on land, and they still manage to overcome him. Crying for the crew aboard ship to hoist him above, Jeff is left to fend for the now recovered diamonds. The sight of seeing the walking dead underwater attacking men in driver's suits is quite eerie and frightening. A similar effect is achieved when the humans discover the hidden zombie mausoleum where 10 zombies occupy 10 coffins, but they come to re-animated life when the humans arrive. Thus, *Zombies of Mora Tau* does have a few highpoints, but much of the movie is very slow-paced, talky and visually dull.

However, this four-film Sam Katzman box set only attests to the fact that many B movies of merit were produced during the 1950s that were not produced by AIP, Allied Artists and other better-known releasing/production companies. These Columbia programmers are worthy of re-evaluation, and as viewed in these pristine and widescreen prints (only the earlier-produced *Creature With the Atom Brain* appears in the 4:3 format), they never looked better. The package even comes with a two-reel comedy short and Mr. Magoo cartoon.

Crypt of the Vampire
Movie: 2.5; Disc: 3.0
RetroMedia

When it comes to mid-1960s drive-in theater Italian/French/Spanish film fare, it seemed, when I was a child, that one was just as good as all the rest. As time moves on it is apparent that Euro movies such as *Castle of Blood*, *The Horrible Dr. Hichcock* and *The Whip and the Body* are superior to others such as this one, *Crypt of the Vampire*. Of course it helps to have Barbara Steele in the cast, which *Crypt of the Vampire* does not. However, even the presence of Christopher Lee playing another one of his haughty, aristocratic roles (as Count Karnstein, no less) adds little to the production, except for his chiseled, handsome features.

Crypt of the Vampire suffers from all the European cinema clichés. The film presents mood (the film was photographed at an actual Gothic castle)—dripping fog and shadowy night photography, some of it day-for-night—over plot. So little happens for so much of the movie. When director Carmillo Mastrocinque (Americanized in the U.S. version as Thomas Miller) decides to make something happen visually, he does an outstanding job for the most part. Stealing from the best, Mario Bava's *Black Sunday* primarily, Mastrocinque features dream sequences from the viewpoint of Laura (Adriana Ambesi), who sees herself as an ancestral witch tied naked to a wooden cross (her body faces the cross and she is allowed to wear black shorts) … her final words declare she will avenge the ancestors of everyone who condemned her to death. In the present time, demonstrating not much has changed, she is lying naked on the castle dungeon floor, spread eagle, again wearing shorts, atop a five-pointed star. The strange housekeeper puts Laura through this torture to try to determine the cause of the local evil, where victims are found drained of all blood. The locals fear that this ancient witch, Sira von Karnstein, is back, gaining revenge. All signs point to Laura's demonic possession, and the young, hauntingly beautiful brunette is watched closely. Also watched is her blonde and equally beautiful friend Lyuba (Ursula Davis), who protects Laura from the forces of evil. But by the film's end the blonde's alternate identity is revealed. Of course during the film's climax, as Laura's potential young male suitor and Count Karnstein search for a hidden painting revealing the identity of the evil witch, the two sexy women, arm in arm, frolic in the darkness of night on the grounds surrounding the castle. Both women are clad in white nightgowns, suggesting a physical relationship may exist between the two soul mates. Down in the forbidden dungeon of Karnstein's castle, the Count invites the young man to stay behind, but the suitor wants to follow along to discover the secret of evil that has haunted the Karnstein family for generations. This leads to the money sequence focusing on a glass-covered metal coffin, housing a Karnstein ancestor (strangely the corpse is perfectly intact and well preserved) who suddenly springs to life, attacking the young suitor from behind. And then the corpse of the witch is found. Of course the hero will use something metallic and sharp to pierce her chest, this blood ritual killing her reincarnated human counterpart. But is the demon possessed victim Laura, or it is her blonde companion Lyuba? What little suspense and secrets the film offers will not be revealed here.

While not one of the best of its ilk, *Crypt of the Vampire* does feature wonderfully moody black-and-white photography, and the few exciting sequences are generally worth waiting for. Unfortunately too little happens for much of the film's running time and this boredom works against the merits of the film. No extras are included except for a RetroMedia website link, but the print used is quite nice and the most complete version of this title yet released.

The Giant Behemoth
Movie: 3.0; Disc: 3.5
Warner Bros.

When it comes to the giant monster movies of the 1950s, we look to the AIP work of Bert I. Gordon, Universal-International films such as *Tarantula,* and of course the masterful work created by Ray Harryhausen. Sometimes forgotten is the latter-day work of Willis O'Brien (the glory days of *King Kong, Son of Kong* and *Mighty Joe Young* were long gone) and collaborator Pete Peterson (who worked with O'Brien as second technician on *Mighty Joe Young*; Harryhausen was first technician), *The Black Scorpion* and *The Giant Behemoth*. Working with low budgets and very little time, these monster matinees created by O'Brien and Peterson are better than generally remembered, featuring cleverly conceived special effects.

When it came to the highly praised Harryhausen black-and-white productions, movies such as *Beast from 20,000 Fathoms* and *20 Million Miles to Earth* spring to memory immediately. The polished cinematic wizardry of Harryhausen was on the ascent, with his best work before him; Willis O'Brien no longer had the clout or the major studio financing behind him during the 1950s, so fans are quick to dismiss any of O'Brien's stop-motion animation work after *Mighty Joe Young*. Even Bela Lugosi fans find magic in his latter films such as *Bride of the Monster* and *Bela Lugosi Meets a Brooklyn Gorilla*. And for fans of O'Brien, we can hail *The Giant Behemoth* as a solid and well-produced B dinosaur romp.

First, many rightfully claim the similarities of *The Giant Behemoth* and *The Beast from 20,000 Fathoms*, but any movie where a dinosaur is let loose in a major metropolitan area, with panicking people being consumed, is bound to share visual commonalities. And while both dinosaurs are similar in design, one must give the

edge to Harryhausen's work. However, the radiation-spewing O'Brien dinosaur is deftly executed and most of the set pieces used to demonstrate the monster's destruction of London are well handled. In one instance a ferryboat carrying people and cars is gliding across a river, when the monster is sighted and rears its head above water. As filmed, the sequence generates both tension and horror with effective editing sea-sawing between reaction shots of people screaming, those being burned by the radiation the monster emits (making such sequences closer to Toho's *Godzilla* than to the Harryhausen monsterfest), and the wonderful effects shots showing the monster's attack upon the floating vessel. By the end of the sequence, people are jumping into the water to save their lives, as the monster upends the ferry and plops cars and people downward to their death. Such a sequence is well handled in all departments, and both children and adults are getting their money's worth.

One of the major flaws of these early Harryhausen movies is the overabundance of American military might that often slows down the plot and relegates most of the monster antics to the third act. Harryhausen's *It Came from Beneath the Sea* is most guilty of such crimes. However, *The Giant Behemoth* focuses on American scientist Steve Karnes (Gene Evans from TV's *My Friend Flicka*) teaming with British scientist Professor James Bickford (Andre Morell, Peter Cushing's Watson in the same year's *The Hound of the Baskervilles*) and showing how their mutual friendship solves the problem and saves the world, at least temporarily. To me, under Eugene Lourie's direction, this British-produced movie most resembles the Val Guest Quatermass movies, produced by Hammer. *The Giant Behemoth* is a talky movie, but so were the Quatermass productions. *The Giant Behemoth* is based upon a brooding sense of mystery that intensifies as the movie unravels, and the repartee between the leads, as they attempt to solve the cause of dead radiation victims and massive fish kills that rot on the English rural beaches, somehow amplifies the tension. Yes, most of the monster antics appear in the final act of the movie, but the script, cinematography and direction keep the audience on the edge of their seat during the first two acts. In fact the original script was embellished to include a giant monster only after the producers turned that story down. When viewers see that glowing, pulsating radioactive blob on the beach shortly after the elderly fisherman is found near death, burned to a crisp, well, that was the only type of monster in the original script. Producers felt that beachside blob could not carry the entire movie, so they demanded a dinosaur be added.

So, bottom line, *The Giant Behemoth* may lack some of the production values and special effects work created by Ray Harryhausen, but the effects created by O'Brien and Peterson come very close to equaling Harryhausen's vision. And having the film's location be Great Britain, with wonderful cinematography focusing upon the gloomy, cloudy and desolated English landscape, only adds another dimension of dread and gloom. O'Brien and team create long stretches of monster mayhem and the framing story always remains interesting. Warner Bros. has released a razor-sharp and densely contrasted print that makes the film's presentation sparkle. *The Giant Behemoth* is ready for its well-deserved re-evaluation.

The Host
Movie: 3.5; Disc: 4.0
Magnolia

During the decades of the 1950s and 1960s, imaginative, giant monsters were everywhere. Even if no better than

a stuntman in a rubber suit, a plethora of hideous and frightening monsters abounded on cinema screens from coast to coast. In today's cinema, the monster is a rare commodity indeed. However, Korea has created a wonderful monster of its own, one that is far better than anyone might have imagined. Using state of the art visual effects (of the most dazzling CGI variety), *The Host* becomes, for this age, what *Godzilla* was to the post-war atomic age. Here the monster is a product of toxic dumping of chemicals (dusty bottles used in autopsies, no less, that are poured down the drain), a virtual "save the planet from pollution" plea. If *Godzilla* warned the world of the dangers of unbridled nuclear energy, the monster of *The Host* warns of the dangers inherent in tainting our formerly pure rivers and waterways.

The monster here is pure animal, pure predator ... there's not a hint of human intelligence within (as was true of the creature from *Alien*). This monster is awkward on land. When the crowds assemble along the Han River to see the black form of the monster first flop from the girders of a bridge into the waters below, resembling goopy sludge or industrial waste more so than a mutated amphibian, they start to throw cans of beer and trashy snacks into the water to attract the animal's attention. When the monster gets the pleasant smell of human flesh, it emerges on land and chases human prey on its shaky legs, stuffing as many people as possible into its hydra-like multiple mouths (sequences of peoples' legs or torsos hanging from the mouth are eerie and disturbing). Bystanders use signs held in cement bases to whack the creature and disturb its feeding frenzy, but the monster always recovers, regroups and traps more innocent victims. In one spectacular sequence, the monster advances so quickly that a beautiful girl finds herself ripped by the hair across the lawn as the monster runs away at breakneck speed. It's a very effective sequence, quite surprising.

Unlike the typical giant monster film of the 1950s (and this beast, while huge, is more the size of a rhinoceros; it's not gigantic), the film offers plenty of set pieces involving the monster's attacks and its habits in its under-the-bridge lair. And unlike the earlier monster mash epics, the plot is developed carefully and features more than scientists and the military trying to find that super weapon that could destroy the beast. Besides its obvious "green" theme, the plot focuses upon a typically dysfunctional middle-class family. The elder single-parent father runs a food stand, a kiosk, along the Han River, and works with his slacker son, who has fits of simply falling asleep at the most inopportune times. That son is raising, alone, a young daughter, a child of about 10 or so, who adores her father and they bond by drinking cans of beer. A younger brother, more handsome, always insults his older brother and calls him retarded, while a sister achieves fame as a competitive archer (foreshadowing the film's conclusion, of course). The plot's crisis is established quickly when the slacker father, who has done some pretty heroic stunts in fighting off the monster during its initial Han River attack, thinks he is grabbing his own daughter's hand and flees, but he sadly finds out that he has the wrong child and his own daughter is defenseless and soon snatched up by the tail of the monster and taken into the river, when the monster is well fed and ready to return to its lair. While the daughter is alive, she is dumped with other living but injured victims in the concrete lair where the monster stores its food for future feedings. The movie basically involves the family's efforts to rescue the child.

But there's more to this complex plot. It seems that the government and military think people who come into close contact with the monster (the slacker father's face is splashed with blood) are infected with an unknown plague/virus, so the entire family is quarantined and arrested by the military police. Probed with needles with doctors drilling into his skull, the slacker son wishes that he and his family could be free to search for his daughter. So these authority figures become monsters, along with the actual predatory beast. The family is on the run from everything and everyone. Amazingly, director Joon-ho Bong (not yet 30 years old) uses the synergy between the family members to create many family moments, comedic ones, frightening ones and gut-wrenchingly tender ones. While the monster is always the chief focus, this whacky Korean family engages our interest and emotions, thus becoming the primary reason why *The Host* is a superior monster movie.

During the movie's climax the determined young father and brother pull two children's bodies from the mouth of the monster (unfortunately, one living boy and one dead daughter), suggesting the imagery of *Little Red Riding Hood* or *Jonah and the Whale*. A fight to the death occurs upon the bridge, where college students are protesting the use of Agent Yellow, as huge chemical smoke bombs are released to fight the non-existent plague. The monster smells human prey and becomes land-borne for the final time. The archery-wielding sister uses a fiery arrow to torch the gasoline-drenched beast, and when it runs for the cooling river water, the father intervenes and shoves a metal shaft down its throat, finally killing the monster. With superior surround sound and impressive sub-woofer tones, this ultimate battle rivals the similar one between the Anglo Saxon-created Beowulf and Grendel.

Interestingly, after the daughter is buried and properly grieved, our slacker father and his newly adopted son sit at the dining room table to have a peaceful meal with the TV blaring the latest news broadcast of the world's horrors in the background. With subtle determination, the child asks the father to turn off the TV so they can concentrate on their meal. And with such a quiet ending, the little boy speaks for all of us when he demands that we finally switch off the horrors of the outside world, turn off all our intrusive media, and instead concentrate on the intimate pleasures of sharing a quiet family meal and enjoying the pleasures of each other's company.

Besides providing a superb print (both dubbed into English and in the original language with subtitles), a second disc is included containing hours of documentaries about every aspect of the film: directing, scripting, storyboarding, casting, creating the visual effects, the actual production itself, etc. Seldom has so much information been shared in so many well-made documentary making-of films. *The Host* proves that fresh blood can be found in the monster-running-amok movie, and that by focusing upon a story that is family oriented, the giant monster movie be elevated and energized once again.